HISTORIC HAUNTS OF SUMNER COUNTY, TENNESSEE

HISTORIC HAUNTS OF SUMNER COUNTY, TENNESSEE

DONNA LYN HARTLEY

Published by Haunted America
A Division of The History Press
Charleston, SC
www.historypress.com

First published 2022

Manufactured in the United States

ISBN 9781467144117

Library of Congress Control Number: 2021952408

For my mother, Mary Mae McDonald Hartley, who introduced me to the excitement of covering breaking news and the reward of developing a multilayered feature story.

To my dad, Harry H. Hartley, artist/illustrator, who allowed me to roam his office, the local newspaper, from a young age, soaking up every facet of producing the printed word.

CONTENTS

Contents

Acknowledgments

Thank you to the people who have made the Gallatin Ghost Walk a sixteen-year success story as one of the first history/mystery tour venues in Tennessee.

Those who shared a story for this book deserve my heartfelt thanks.

Many encouraged me throughout this endeavor, but most especially, this book could not have been written without the help of historians Randy P. Lucas and Jerry Lumpkins.

Barry "Bear" Gaunt and Melvin Brazzell of Night Stalkers Paranormal Research introduced me to "high strangeness" and helped me put names and context to some of the unexplainable things that occur in Sumner County.

Gentlemen, your input was priceless—and so is your continued friendship.

Bryan Roehrig, interviewed in chapter three, passed away shortly after he graciously gave his account of the paranormal activity in his law office for inclusion in this book. The legal community has lost a great friend. Bryan was compassionate and helpful to clients and other attorneys. His devotion to animal welfare in Sumner County will also be missed.

A fire gutted Hancock House, the circa-1830 log structure detailed in chapter 6, as this book went into production.

INTRODUCTION

Sumner County, Tennessee, exemplifies the spirit of the young, postcolonial America on many diverse and colorful levels.

The early 1700s saw long hunters brave the unknown wilds of the Cumberland Plateau to trap and hunt animals whose skins and furs made the hats and garments worn by the fashionable in burgeoning eastern American cities.

Later, men who had fought the British in the American Revolution came to this area of Tennessee (then part of North Carolina) on land grants, seeking success and adventure in what was then the Wild West.

Individuals who would become American icons, notably Andrew Jackson, a young circuit riding district attorney who once had an office on the Gallatin Public Square and owned a general store here; Sam Houston, who entered into a mysterious marriage with a local woman, the dissolution of which two weeks after the nuptials remains a mystery to this day; and Civil War cavalry legend John Hunt Morgan, all put their stamp on the personality of the region and the world.

These illustrious men and their families—and others like them, whose names are not legend but who established the foundation for a prosperous future—found a lush landscape, plenty of water and land whose mineral content gave their livestock particularly strong bones, just as the leisure pastime of the new nation, Thoroughbred breeding and horse racing, was in its infancy.

And thus began the fifty-plus years of the Tennessee gentleman horse farmer and horses that would make racing history. The lavish lifestyle of the racing world and the elegant architecture of Sumner County's opulent horse farms would put the area on the map as the center of the American racing world and the epitome of the style and grace that became the southern way—until the Civil War ended it all.

There were no major battles in Sumner County—unless you count the private war civilians waged daily under the brutal occupation of a Union general who decided to make Sumner County an example for any other Rebels who would dare step out of line.

One young woman, Alice Williamson, wrote a diary of the times.

The first entry begins, "It was a good day today in Gallatin; nobody was hanged."

Sumner County's dramatic and fascinating history has given us some of the most interesting (and terrifying) hauntings one is likely to find anywhere: from the demonic to the merely mysterious, our captivating spirits have a story to tell for those who are brave enough to listen.

1
CRAGFONT
PORTAL TO THE PARANORMAL

*The old baronial Cragfont…like a medieval castle on the Rhine or Mose…
overlooking Bledsoe's Creek, that famous stream that came pouring its crystal
waters from the spurs of the Cumberland Mountains.*
—John Hallum

"STAY OUT OF THERE"

The priest came at the request of an old friend and ex-parishioner. Traveling from Ohio to middle Tennessee to bless a house was a little outside of the duties of even the most dedicated priest, but his friend had been named to the board of directors of a home of distinct historical significance known as Cragfont that was being extensively renovated and would eventually be open to the public.

According to the priest's friend, the house had always been a bit of a problem when vacant, as it had been a hangout spot for kids wanting to drink and party, vagrants and those who wanted to find out if it was—as had been reported for almost one hundred years—haunted. And, she revealed, the committee tasked with organizing the renovations had had a little "trouble" of their own: a psychic they had employed to investigate the house had reported, "This place is loaded [with spirits], and they are unhappy you're here."

It was 1981, and Lowell Fayna, present for both the psychic's visit and the priest's, had just been hired, along with his wife, Kim, to be the onsite caretaker of the property, living in the little house behind the main structure that would soon see its own share of paranormal activity. "We had already had some trouble at the main house," said Fayna. "Lights had been going off and on, impressions had been left on a just-made-up bed while no one was in the room. A broadax had been flung at me across a room," thrown by unseen hands. And a sulfur smell often permeated the three-story structure, said Fayna.

Enter the priest from Ohio, who, after coming into the home, immediately asked for a glass of water. Fayna, a Southern Baptist, thought he was thirsty and offered him a Coke instead. "Not to drink," smiled the priest. "To bless." Fayna complied.

The priest walked slowly and deliberately through the house, sprinkling each room with water, made recently holy by his own blessing. He took a few steps up the stairs that led to the ballroom and nursery but stopped, breathing hard. "He completely lost his breath," recalled Fayna. "We had to get one person on either side of him and help him outside....He kept saying 'I'm okay, I'm okay,' but he was weak and pale....When he had regained his breath, he told us, 'Those things are demonic; you need to stay out of there as much as possible.'"

Stay out? Stay out of a home recently acquired by the State of Tennessee in anticipation of it becoming a jewel in the crown of historic homes not just in the area but in the state and even the South? Stay out of a significant architectural structure with a rich and storied past that had absolutely nothing to do with anything paranormal or evil?

"We had no choice but to carry on and deal with whatever we faced on our own," said Fayna. "Maybe whatever it was would go away."

A Manse on the Wild Frontier

When we think of the "Wild West," we think of "cowboys and Indians," California gold prospectors, tumbleweeds and gunfights.

But for a young America, the Revolutionary War brought freedom from the English. And never content with the status quo, Americans, who, at their core, are risk takers and prospectors for what they cannot see beyond the next horizon, wanted more. Having just taken on the most powerful army in the world—that of Great Britain—what was left but to strike out for parts unknown, and win them, too?

The Wild West in the late 1700s was the land west of the Allegheny Mountains, and the untamed expanse of Tennessee (part of North Carolina until 1796) was virgin territory just waiting to be explored and conquered.

Into this unexplored (at least by White men) unknown came men who would become legend: Andrew Jackson, Sam Houston, John Sevier, James Robertson and Cragfont's own James Winchester. Many of these men had moved west on land grants given to them for their service to the colonies in their bid for autonomy.

Architect J. Frazer Smith, who visited Cragfont in the late 1930s and included it in his book *White Pillars, A Survey of Southern Dwellings of the First Half of the 1800s*, called the structure "a typical glorified pioneer dwelling executed in native stone....A visit to Cragfont is equivalent to reading a page from cultural and architectural history, for this fine old pioneer home illustrates the evolution of a natural plan of building on the frontier."

"Here, a man came from the old world of custom and refinement [and] adjusted himself to keep step with a backwoods settlement....[This homestead was] typical of the period, as sturdily indigenous as the virgin

Architect J. Frazer Smith described the majestic hilltop Cragfont as "typical of the period, as sturdily indigenous as the virgin timber and native stone that went into [its] construction... [portraying] frontier society at its height." *Author's collection.*

timber and native stone that went into [its] construction…[portraying] frontier society at its height," wrote Smith.

A neighbor of the Winchesters, John Hallum, described the house in his memoirs *Diary of An Old Lawyer*, published in 1895 by Southwestern Publishing House, as "the old baronial Cragfont…[towering] like a medieval castle on the Rhine or Mose…overlooking Bledsoe's Creek, that famous stream that came pouring its crystal waters from the spurs of the Cumberland mountains."

Indeed, Cragfont's builder and first occupant, James Winchester, was a Baltimore native of impeccable lineage. Born into an aristocratic family of English origins in Carroll County, Maryland, in 1752, Winchester distinguished himself in the Revolutionary War under Generals Washington and Greene and enthusiastically took advantage of the offer of a land grant in new territory, available to war veterans who had seen meritorious service and were willing to brave the perils of the wilderness to establish settlements beyond the Allegheny Mountains. To the victors belonged the spoils of an uncharted new world, and these intrepid individuals and their families left comfortable homes and established communities back east on an unparalleled adventure that is uniquely American in its scope and quest.

Such a journey involved entire families and all their worldly goods sailing on flatboats down the Tennessee River in East Tennessee and then up the Cumberland River. It was an arduous journey, involving battles with Natives who were hostile to westward expansion by White settlers, disease, harsh weather and treacherous waters. Some two hundred families preceding the Winchesters had followed just that route to establish Nashville some five years prior. The danger of the Native populations was not exaggerated: in 1785, most of the middle Tennessee White populations lived in forts, which were constantly under siege.

But not James Winchester.

By 1785, he had staked out his claim to a "fine site on a creek a mile from Bledsoe's Station, amid a native forest full of game and crossed by Indian trails. Within three years, he built a large mill, married a charming young lady of the county, and established a home," wrote Smith. "The long drive up a dangerous and rocky lane from the highway to Cragfont is a fitting introduction to what is to come at the end of the drive. Situated at the very top of the craggy hill above Bledsoe's Creek, the house looks down on the approaching visitor with all of the hauteur and dignity befitting the position of eminence occupied by its builder," Smith added.

Left: Susan Black Winchester. *Right*: General James Winchester. *Courtesy of the Tennessee State Library and Archives.*

Smith described an "enormous ballroom, probably the first in a private home in the state. There is a remarkable resemblance in the plan location of this ballroom to that of the Governor's Palace in Williamsburg. Members of the old families in the Nashville section still recount stories of ladies and gentlemen dancing out through the doors of the ballroom on to the porches to seek romance in the soft light of a summer moon, while the strains of violins floated over the fragrant gardens." It is on these porches that, even today, guests at weddings and parties held on Cragfont grounds will see a petite, dark-haired woman in a long, blue gown, strolling up and down the galleried walkway, observing the crowd—a woman who disappears in a white mist if one gazes at her too long.

Winchester's military acumen was "invaluable to the early settlers [of Middle Tennessee], directing the scouts and spies and frequently pursuing the Indians in person, showing himself at all times a true and prudent officer," said Edward Albright in his *Early History of Middle Tennessee.*

Winchester would, again, distinguish himself as an officer in the War of 1812, where his friendship with Andrew Jackson solidified. In fact, militia troops from Middle Tennessee trained on the grounds of Cragfont.

During that war, Winchester received a general's commission and "was ordered to take command of one wing of the army of the northwest. At the unfortunate Battle of the River Raisin [in what is now Michigan], he was taken prisoner by the British and carried to Quebec, where he remained in captivity during the following winter," said Albright.

Illustrious visitors to an early Cragfont included future American legends such as Lafayette, Aaron Burr and Sam Houston, who would marry a local girl, Eliza Allen, only to be divorced two weeks later—one of the most notorious scandals of the times. This unfortunate and short liaison would result in Houston being burned in effigy on the county courthouse square in nearby Gallatin. He then resigned as the governor of Tennessee and fled to live with the Natives for several years prior to riding into Texas—and history.

Winchester founded the city of Memphis and was prominent in many phases of frontier life through a mercantile business and steamboat interests.

He died at his beloved home in 1826, but his wife would live another forty years as mistress of the house, dying in 1864 at the age of eighty-seven.

Origins of Phenomena

Lowell Fayna ended his forty-year career at Cragfont shortly after unseen hands placed a noose around his neck as he made his early morning rounds at the historic plantation.

Fayna and his wife, Kim, lived on the grounds of Cragfont for most of the years Fayna was associated with the site, and during that time, he saw more paranormal activity than many diehard ghost hunters will see in a lifetime.

Fayna is not alone in seeing spectres and being personally accosted or confronted by the entities at Cragfont.

"When people come up and say, 'Lowell, you're gonna think I'm crazy but—' I know what's coming," Fayna said with a wry grin that is boyish and mischievous under his brushy white mustache, despite his eighty-plus years.

A native of Virginia, as a young man, Lowell Fayna was a musician, first in his home state and then in Nashville. In later years—and concurrent with living at Cragfont—he served as a sheriff's deputy. He doesn't shy away from a fight, is plainspoken and stands over six feet tall without a stoop, despite his age. He maintains a strong Christian faith and is involved with various projects to aid and assist the less fortunate in the area.

"My wife, Kim, and I came to Cragfont as a couple to live on the grounds and for her to serve as director of the historic home while I was working for the Sumner County Sheriff's Department, as well as overseeing day-to-day operations at Cragfont," explained Fayna, adding, "Cragfont was a job that was to last for thirty-eight years. Kim died in 2015, and I spent three more years there as tour guide and general groundskeeper."

Fayna took the loss of his wife hard. "I had spent so much time at Cragfont with her, side by side, and living on the grounds those many years, I just lost the heart for it [Cragfont] when she died. It was time to retire."

Cragfont was acquired by the State of Tennessee in 1952 and was opened to the public in 1962. But it was not until 1981, when Fayna came on the scene, that efforts to make the home a premier historic site became serious.

"Rosemary Rogers was the president of the Cragfont board, and she instructed me on one of my very first days there at Cragfont, 'I'm going to caution you, and I don't want you to get scared, but this place is haunted,'" Fayna remembered. "Well, I'm one of those guys that has to see it to believe it, and, I guess, by God, I did, but at that time, I thought, 'Yeah right,'" he said.

> *Mrs. Rogers said, "I want us to get together and come up with a way to get those haunts out of there." Well, that's when she brought in the priest and that didn't work out. Me and my wife were naive about ghosts and demons and such, and, as I would find out later was a huge mistake, my wife started fooling around with a Ouija board, and she and other board members and friends would get out the Ouija board and start asking the "ghosts" questions.*
>
> *I seem to remember they weren't getting much you could really decipher out of those Ouija board sessions, but I do remember this: one day, Mrs. Rogers came up there to the house, and we were standing on the front lawn, and she said right out loud, as if speaking to the house itself and any paranormal "occupants," "I want you out of my house." You can't believe the racket that started. It sounded like the tin roof was collapsing around us, as if it were being ripped from the house and shook. We ran. I mean* ran *to our cars.*

The entities had laid down the gauntlet. For Lowell Fayna and his wife, the activity in their house, which was located on the property, commenced shortly thereafter and resulted in an incident that finally drove them from the property and into their own home some miles away from Cragfont, to safety—at least during the nighttime hours. And the paranormal activity inside the house became prevalent and disturbing.

In his duties as a sheriff's deputy, Fayna carried a gun and brought it home with him every night after work, laying it on his dresser but keeping it loaded. "A deputy's gun is serious business. We are considered 'undressed' without it," said Fayna.

Lowell Fayna was the site director for Historic Cragfont for almost forty years, overseeing its restoration and living on the grounds for much of that time. He experienced firsthand much of the paranormal activity that occurs in the over-two-hundred-year-old structure. *Author's collection.*

> *One morning, I got up and dressed, and my gun was nowhere to be found. I had to go to work without and receive a serious bawling out for not having it on my person. It's part of my equipment.*
>
> *My wife and I got into a tiff about it; I accused her of doing something with my weapon, and she denied it. We simply couldn't find an explanation.*
>
> *It reappeared, but then a couple of weeks later, my badge went missing for a couple of days.*
>
> *By that point, I was pretty sure what I was dealing with. Something was messing with my stuff. This was probably the first time I started hollering out loud to "whoever" was listening: "I gotta have my gun, and my badge, stop messing with them!"*
>
> *But I did unload my weapon at night from then on.*

Concurrently, Fayna started experiencing the beginning of what was to be long years of having things thrown at him by unseen hands. "In the wine room, on the wall, hangs a broadax from the time of the building of the house. It is a primitive tool, and it's heavy and dangerous to play around with. One day, that thing went whizzing by my head while I was by myself in that room," Fayna recounted.

"During this period, my wife and her friends continued to play with the Ouija board, and then another strange communication began. Orbs of light would float about the room, particularly in the nursery next to the ballroom, and my wife would talk to them, and they would respond with vigorous activity as if trying to answer."

Some of the physical evidence of the hauntings is difficult to ignore, much less to explain.

"We keep red checkered tablecloths in the sideboard drawers for some of the outdoor events," Fayna said. Fayna hated the evergreen trees that lined the walkway in the front of the house and cut them down one summer day. The next day, when he unlocked the house, the red checkered tablecloths had been draped over all the windows facing the walkway. "I guess 'they' didn't like the summer sun that was now flooding through the windows—that's all I can think of," said Fayna. "It's just one of those things we can't explain."

Every year that Lowell Fayna worked at the historic home, Cragfont hosted an open house the first Sunday of December. "I'd work real hard cutting down an evergreen tree from the property and bringing it in to decorate.... The house would be beautiful and festive and decorated to a T. It wasn't unusual to leave the room for a minute only to return and everything had been torn down or otherwise messed up."

"One year, just before the open house, I was walking up the stairs, and as I got to the landing where an antique grandfather clock stands, the clock's door face fell off and hit me in the head, drawing blood. It didn't just fall off; its hinges were twisted," Fayna recalled.

"We also have permanent grooves in the floor from the very heavy harpsichord that moves across the room on a regular basis....It takes four men to lift that thing. Who's moving it in the night between the time I lock up and the time I get here in the morning to open up?" Fayna asked as he pondered these strange events, even these many years later.

And then there's the telephone.

The landline has been known to call 911 all by itself. Currently, there is no landline in the house, and the caretaker on the property lives at his own residence about seventy-five yards from the house—with his own cellphone. Nevertheless, 911 still occasionally receives a call from the old, disconnected landline number.

While Fayna was still at Cragfont daily, two heavy oil portraits of Winchester family members, measuring four feet by eight feet, were occasionally known to be off their hooks and sitting on the floor when Fayna opened in the mornings. "Those things are heavy, and it takes two people to hang them," he said.

"'They' have moved a solid-wood, glass-fronted wardrobe from one room to the other, an antique piece that takes two men to wrangle. Guests at parties have had candles thrown at them from the chandeliers. People will call after they visit the house, get home and get the nerve to call me and say, 'Lowell, something touched me in that house.'"

During the 2007 tornado that leveled the historic Wynnewood structure about a mile from Cragfont, Fayna rushed out to Cragfont to see if the house had been spared or if it was part of the massive destruction that was being reported from all over Sumner County. He found the locked house still standing and perfectly secure, but all the dining room chairs had been moved. Each window downstairs had a chair in front of it, as if someone had been watching the storm pass.

"I've had twelve pairs of glasses knocked off my face by unseen hands—and not just knocked off but twisted. I've smoothed the master bedroom bedspread and walked out of the room, only to return a few minutes later to see either the imprint of a person on the bed, or a book from the library lying there open and face down, along with the imprint. They are fond of *The History of England, Volume One*," said Fayna with a smile.

"I had begun to figure that I pissed them off early on by refusing to be a part of the Ouija board sessions; plus, I would challenge them—very much like the day Mrs. Rogers bellowed, 'Leave my house alone!' and it sounded like the sky fell in. I would holler at them, 'Come on, boys, I'll take you out,' and macho stuff like that. I think that was a mistake."

"One summer day, while cutting the grass on my John Deere tractor, my cap was yanked off my head. There wasn't a wind; it was a hot, still summer day. I looked around—no cap in sight. I went on and mowed and came back around to my starting point, and there was the cap lying on the ground—on fire," Fayna said.

It got worse.

"Something actually took the wheel of my tractor while I was mowing and ran me into the pond. The tractor was completely out of my control. I can't possibly describe to you how it felt....It simply went out of my control, but I knew I was keeping the wheel straight. I nearly resigned right then, because what was I going to tell the State of Tennessee, who owns the house? Ghosts turned the wheel and wrecked their $10,000 piece of machinery?" recalled Fayna.

It wasn't long after the tractor incident that an occurrence involving Fayna's wife, Kim, became the "last straw" for the couple, who were still living in the little house on the property, directly behind the main house.

"I woke up one morning, and my wife was not in the bed beside me; she had gotten up earlier to make coffee, I supposed, but when she heard me up, she came to me and said, 'Sweetheart, there is something I need to tell you,'" Fayna remembered.

"It was a little early in the morning for serious conversation, and I just kind of muttered, 'What, what's wrong?' Then I could see she was really upset; big tears were coming down. I had to pull the story out of her in bits and pieces. We'd been married a pretty long time, and I'd never seen Kim unable to tell me something," said Fayna.

"I want you to know I'm not crazy," she said.

"I know that, now what's wrong?"

"Lowell, don't laugh now—I mean it," she said.

"'OK, I won't laugh,' I said, but I almost did laugh, but stopped myself because she was still crying," said Fayna, adding, "I knew this was no laughing matter. Then Kim offered to show me what had her so upset," Fayna recalled. "Rolled up nice and neat at the foot of the bed were the pair of panties she had worn to bed the night before, on top of the bedspread, just as she had found them when she woke up."

"Well, I just lost it," Fayna remembered. "This thing was out of hand."

"Kim said, 'I went to bed with my underwear on, and this morning, it was on top of the bedspread.'"

"That was it. We no longer lived on the property. We continued to work there, but no way were we going to live in that house."

In 1987, parts of the movie sequel to the Alex Haley miniseries *Roots* were filmed at Cragfont and on its grounds.

The cast of *Roots: The Gift* included Morgan Freeman, LeVar Burton and Michael Learned, among others, and the scenes took place in winter. It was summertime, so to create a winter wonderland, plastic snow had to be blown onto the ground by way of a big water tanker that the production company had leased from Andrew Jackson's home, the Hermitage, where alternate scenes in the movie were filmed. "I watched them park the tanker on the hill and put large chocks under all four tires; it was secure. As secure as it gets," said Fayna.

In fact, with Hollywood stars on the set and big money being spent on a sequel to one of the most acclaimed miniseries of all time, security was tight and prominent. The public was not allowed to wander around the sets or Cragfont during filming.

"Wouldn't you just know, late in the production, that tanker rolled down the hill into Bledsoe's Creek, tearing out several trees, and was wrecked," lamented Fayna. "The chocks hadn't just slipped. We found them halfway down the hill," said Lowell. The movie's production budget had to reimburse the Hermitage for its tanker.

It was another expensive bit of mischief—just like the tractor and pond incidents.

Julie Fagen Allen grew up in the county and "must have been to Cragfont one hundred times." "As a small child, I heard stories that terrified me," Allen said. "Ten years ago, a huge group of bikers came to tour Cragfont while we were visiting the house," Allen remembered. "These big burly guys didn't look like they would be afraid of much of anything, but when they got to the second story," said Allen, "there was a loud knock on one of the windows; of course, no one was there. The bikers hit the stairs, and I was so scared, I ran, leaving my ten-year-old child temporarily behind."

None of these spirit manifestations involve actual apparitions, except for two: Susan Winchester and the Confederate soldier who was seen by Fayna and a gardener one late spring day.

"I looked up one morning from my tractor to see a Confederate soldier walking across the lawn," said Fayna. "He had a rifle; he was in full Army of Tennessee soldier apparel. 'Well,' I said, 'hold up, hoss,' and he stopped. He turned around, dropped his weapon to his side and then disappeared before my eyes."

"Later that morning, a garden committee member who had been working in the yard approached me and said, 'Lowell, I need to tell you something you're just not going to believe.…A Confederate soldier just walked across the road.' She described exactly what I had seen earlier—down to the detail of the man dropping his weapon down to his side upon seeing her."

"Once or twice a week, something like that would happen. Many of these things are on film—on the security camera," Fayna revealed. This includes the incident that finally sent Lowell Fayna into retirement.

"I was vacuuming, and carrying the vacuum downstairs from the ballroom, I felt something hit me on the neck. It is impossible to convey to you how frightening this was, because I immediately brushed at my neck to see what it was, and it was a rope," Fayna said. It was a rope that had been tied into a noose.

> *Now, I'm an old boy scout, and I tell you it was a noose with an intricate knot I had never even seen before. I had that long to look at it, and because I was so astonished, I could hardly bear to look to see what was at the other end of that noose, but when I did look up, it was just suspended in air.*

> *When a noose goes around your neck, and you think you are alone in the house, all sorts of things go through your mind. I am not ashamed to tell you that is the most frightened I have ever been in my life, and I was in law enforcement, so that's saying something.*

After years of confronting the unseen tormenters, challenging them to stop and yelling into the air for them to leave the house and him alone, Lowell Fayna had had enough.

He snatched the rope away from his neck, threw it down and resigned.

"I never even told my girls what had happened," he recalled. "But I will tell you this: the rope incident was caught on the security camera. You can plainly see an arm, attached to nothing, holding that rope."

The Lady of the House

Most haunted historic homes can tie their manifestations to a specific individual who lived in the house or to an occurrence—usually tragic—that seems to be the genesis of an apparition or disturbance.

The only "spirit" at Cragfont that is regularly seen and is directly related to former residents or happenings is the ghost of Susan Black Winchester, the original mistress of the plantation, who lived there and gave birth to fourteen children there.

For over sixty years, she was the mistress of this profitable, working plantation and gathering place for men and women who live forever in our history books.

Susan Black had come to Tennessee as a child, when the territory was still a part of North Carolina, in the early 1780s.

At that time, most settlers, including Susan Black's family, were still living in forts, and Natives were challenging the newcomers' presence on the land with extreme force and brutality. Kidnapping women and scalping children was not unheard of.

An episode at Bledsoe's Lick in Sumner County illustrates that settlers were making every effort to give their children the life they had left behind on the East Coast, but they were under very trying circumstances, as day-to-day life was perilous.

A compact of government had been entered into by the colonists, signed by 256 members, of which only one was unable to write his own name. This indicates that most of the settlers were people of education and therefore had means in the communities from which they had come; they desired for their children to grow up educated, even in the wilds of an unsettled new land.

A schoolmaster, George Hamilton, had been hired to instruct the children at the fort. One night, Hamilton was sitting in Anthony Bledsoe's room, singing at the top of his voice. Natives were prowling around, and one of them found a hole in the back of the chimney, through which he poked his gun and fired, hitting the teacher in the mouth. The teacher recovered, but the incident reveals how, amid attempting civilized endeavors, danger was always at hand.

Susan Winchester's early life in the fort would be in stark contrast to her later life as mistress of Cragfont.

Typical of conditions in the forts, where cabins were separated by stockade enclosures and log blockhouses designed to repel Native attacks, is the account of settlers at Sumner County's Asher's Station. During their first winter, settlers survived mostly on wild game of poor quality, as the deer had died of hunger from heavy snows and intense cold. All food was simple, and the only substitute for butter and lard was bear's oil. A small crop of corn gave them a limited supply of bread come summer.

Only the settlers' constant vigilance kept Natives from attacking, as they viewed the station forts as permanent military establishments. During the day, sentinels were posted to warn of approaching danger. At sunset, the settlers would retire to the blockhouses and their cabins, concealing anything of value within the strong log pickets.

And though survival and finding their next meal was paramount to the settlers, life's happiest moments went on in the form of births and weddings. "The first wedding in the colony [Middle Tennessee] took place at the Bluff during the summer of 1780. It was the marriage of our brave Indian fighter, Captain James Leiper, and the young lady who thus became his wife," wrote Edward Albright.

No minister had yet come to the settlement, and a question arose as to whether any one was authorized to perform the marriage ceremony.

Colonel Robertson, who was chief justice of the court, sent out to the other judges a call for a consultation. It was decided by this court that either of its members, by virtue of his office, was empowered to exercise such a function: the origin of "getting married at city hall" or by certain civil servants so designated by law, that we know of today.

Susan Black and James Winchester were married in 1792. Their marriage was perhaps a common law marriage, and that would not have been unusual.

As noted in the preceding wedding story, ministers were hard to come by on the frontier, but ardent lovers were not deterred by formalities. There are recorded official acts of the Tennessee legislature changing the names of the children born to Susan and James from "Black" to "Winchester" in the years 1803 and 1807. This was the standard method of legitimizing children born in common law marriages.

Fourteen children were born to the Winchesters and bore the name Winchester when all was said and done. Two did not survive infancy and were buried in the formal gardens, while the rest of the family was buried about two hundred yards from the main house.

Cragfont comprised as many as 2,600 acres at the height of its productivity, with twelve slave cabins near the house and as many as one hundred enslaved people working the land and staffing the household.

The mistresses of plantations in Middle Tennessee were far from the "belle" stereotype, with idle hands except for when they were fluttering a lacy fan on a hot summer day or riding sidesaddle at a dainty and ladylike clip. In addition to managing their own family's needs and planning and executing often-elaborate social gatherings, all aspects of the management of the enslaveds' day-to day living, including the supervision of the construction of their homes, clothing and their "official" medical care (for, as we will later note, the enslaved had their own potions, incantations and "spells" against illness), fell to the mistress of the home.

These women had endured incredible challenges as children in the forts and were accomplished horsewomen, riding on horses rather than in carriages. They often spent some part of their days with a neighbor, always traveling to their homes with a small bag on their saddle pommels. Knitting and little bundles of seed were taken out of the bag, carefully opened, and exchanges were made. As the needles began to click, they gossiped about their domestic affairs: gardens, housecleaning, sitting hens, whether chicks had hatched, who had a new calf or a fine filly.

The stacked-stone walls are a typical sight on old homestead farms and plantations in Middle Tennessee and are reminders of the earlier walls of the same style seen all over the British Isles. *Author's collection.*

In 1895, Mr. George W. Gordon, a member of the Memphis bar, reminisced about Susan Winchester.

> *Mrs. James Winchester was possessed of rare personal beauty, strong intellect, and an incredible thirst for knowledge. Cradled in the "block-house" and the fort, her character was molded to the heroic type by the actual happenings of frontier life. Yet, when exigencies of the frontier days passed, she graced the manor as beautifully even as she had blossomed in the wilderness…at the advanced age of eighty-seven, still erect in figure, in the full possession of her mental powers,* [she is] *without bodily infirmity.*

Lowell Fayna said, "Many, many times a guest has come up to me during a party or wedding on the grounds and said, 'Who is the woman in the blue dress?'"

Susan Winchester was buried in a blue dress.

Kristie Owen is a longtime resident of Sumner County, who grew up in a house not far from Cragfont. She was entertaining visitors from Indiana some years ago and took them to tour Cragfont. "We had chills all over from the minute we entered the house," Owen said, "especially in the rooms downstairs….Upstairs, it wasn't any less eerie," she added. "We wanted out."

"Outside, we were okay," Owen said. "We were enjoying the gardens, when we all seemed to turn at the same time to see a woman on the upper-story landing, wearing a long dress...we all saw her and looked at each other. There were no other cars in the parking lot; no one else was there."

"I've been back several times since then and every time, I feel 'something.' I love Cragfont but it's just eerie," Owens laughed.

The Satterwhite Legacy

If Susan Winchester and a lone Confederate soldier are the only "ghosts" seen at Cragfont, then to what may we attribute the almost daily poltergeist-like manifestations experienced by Lowell Fayna for almost forty years?

Long, Long Ago, Reminiscences of Cragfont, by Susan Black Winchester Scales and edited by Ellen Wemyss, Louise Patterson and Sue Botsaris, was printed in the mid-1970s and has had numerous reprintings. The small, twenty-five-page booklet incorporates both an original diary by Susan Scales, the great-granddaughter of Susan Black Winchester, and Nell Satterwhite, who grew up at Cragfont when her father, W.H.B. Satterwhite, owned the property.

Nell not only chronicled her own experiences with the paranormal, but she also interviewed living residents of Sumner County who had recollections and stories of the old homestead. Her writings help give context to Cragfont's history and how its own inhabitants may have contributed to "inviting" activities of a paranormal nature long before Lowell Fayna, his wife and curious others ever consulted the Ouija board in the 1970s.

West African societies, America's largest source of enslaved people, shared a belief in a supreme creator and kept the rites, rituals and cosmologies of Africa alive in America through stories, healing arts, songs and other forms of cultural expression, creating a spiritual space apart from the White European world, even as they embraced the Christianity of their new home.

Cragfont's "semi-official housekeeper, midwife, and official nurse," according to Satterwhite was enslaved and was referred to as "Mammy." "Her power over forces seen and unseen and reputation as a fortune teller and concocter of charms, magic potions and tricks to guard against 'witches' was well-known throughout the neighborhood. Her authority on any point was seldom questioned...[her] cabin, which stood nearest the main house was one of the most haunted spots at Cragfont," long after the enslaved had left the plantation and the cabins were vacant, then torn down. Early in the

Civil War, Middle Tennessee was basically abandoned by the Confederate army, which had been driven out and defeated at such battles as Shiloh and Fort Donelson.

There was little protection for the area's citizenry, as men were away, fighting, and only old men, women and young children were left to tend the home fires against the advancing Union army.

In the fall of 1862, a cruel and malicious general came to take charge of the official occupation of Gallatin and the surrounding areas, including Castalian Springs, where Cragfont is located.

The following occurrence was probably the result of Paine's depredations on the innocent citizens of Sumner County long before Reconstruction ever began and describes an incident that ignited a vengeance so shocking that it may have contributed to some of the paranormal activity of restless spirits.

Nell Satterwhite's diary explains:

> *One morning, Tom, the colored overseer, met with Mrs. Susan Black Winchester....He told her just which portion of Cragfont land and stock he claimed for his own, and just what remained for the Winchesters.*
>
> *As was wont to happen in those days the news of Tom's actions reached the* [Confederate] *"bushwhackers"* [guerrilla soldiers who operated outside the regular army, exacting justice as they saw fit and often preying on sympathizers of the opposing army] *and one morning, a party of masked men called at the plantation.*
>
> *They met Tom, not knowing who he was, and asked him if he knew where "Tom" could be found. Realizing his danger* [Tom] *told them he had seen "Tom" a few minutes earlier going toward the work barn. The bushwhackers headed toward the work barn, and Tom narrowly escaped by running to the river and swimming over to the safety of the Federal agents.*

This infuriated the bushwhackers when they found out they had been hoodwinked. In retaliation, they found Tom's sixteen-year-old son in the Cragfont brick horse barn, kidnapped him and beheaded him in the barn of an adjoining plantation.

The brick horse barn from which the boy was kidnapped was burned to its foundation soon after. A second barn was constructed on the remaining foundation, and it, too, mysteriously burned—as did a third barn. The site gained a reputation in the region for being "haunted."

Years later, when Mr. Satterwhite bought the property, he utilized what remained of the horse barn's dressed stones and bricks and built a large barn. The barn was almost complete when a storm destroyed the structure, along with valuable stock he had put inside.

Some years later, the barn was again replaced. Lightning struck the barn, and more precious stock was burned. A third barn that was constructed was burned "by a fire of unknown origin" said Nell.

One late Easter-time afternoon, Nell and some of her "schoolmates were exploring [the Winchester family cemetery located at the rear of the house], as curious children will do." They "decided to see what was inside of the aboveground old-fashioned tomb. It was rumored to contain a baby's casket; they succeeded in lifting the lid, and sure enough, there was a tiny casket."

> *Not realizing the gravity of their actions and still somewhat skeptical, they lifted out the casket and searched the interior for a button or some other evidence that a human had been buried there. The search for a button was unsuccessful, but they did find a tooth.*
>
> *Over Nell's objections, one of the boys put the tooth in his pocket and teased her about being a scaredy-cat.*
>
> *Later that same evening, everyone was gathered in the parlor, listening to Nell's father tell tales of his youth. He had been showing the group a long-handled gourd* [used for ladling water], *which he placed on the mantel.*
>
> *After some time, the group noticed the since-untouched gourd was rocking slowly and steadily. It continued to rock for several minutes until everyone was pop-eyed in amazement.*
>
> *The gourd was examined to see if a small creature such as a mouse was inside. It was empty, and there was no immediate explanation as to why the gourd rocked in such a rhythmic motion for such a long period of time.*
>
> *One member of the astonished group silently decided he knew the reason for the rocking gourd, and early the next morning, the tooth was replaced in the tiny casket.*
>
> *Nothing more was said about scaredy-cats, and the gourd was at rest.*

Through the years, the Satterwhites and even their guests continued to experience sightings of an apparition resembling Susan Winchester, as well as mysterious silhouettes that would appear in the rooms of the house from time to time.

Some of the more frightening occurrences reported by visitors included being wrapped like a mummy in bedclothes during the night, having mattresses levitate while on them and having pillows snatched from beneath heads.

The Nathaniel Parker log cabin at Bledsoe's Station in Castalian Springs dates to circa 1790 and is typical of the hundreds of log cabins that were built in Sumner County during the era of pioneers. It was a quick way to obtain shelter and protection and was made of poplar, oak, ash and cedar, which were plentiful. *Author's collection.*

Paranormal happenings turned ugly one night, however, when Nell was struck in the mouth while climbing the stairs to the second floor. She was bloody and cut, but the incident was soon dismissed as her simply having stumbled in the dark.

Years later, on a whim, Nell went to a fortune-teller in Nashville who inexplicably told her about her "past" as well as her future, saying, "One night, [that old man] you see in your house tried to 'make way' with you." The fortune-teller, then startled, exclaimed, "Oh, I see blood. It's your mouth—you are bleeding!" This was exactly what had happened to Nell on that stairwell, several years before.

Many nights, Nell and her mother would hear heavy footsteps throughout the house and even heavy furniture being moved about, only to discover on surveillance that nothing was disturbed.

The Satterwhites spent a total of forty-one years at Cragfont.

One of the last and most baffling incidents occurred on a spring morning, when one of Nell's friends passed an open window and glanced out to see a thick, gray cloud rise out of the ground to a height of ten or fifteen feet, fan out "like a bird, spreading its wings…hovered for a moment, then folded in upon itself and slowly returned to the earth, leaving no trace." Nell's friend explained that the "cloud" did not behave as mist would behave; it did not dissipate, rather it appeared to deliberately draw itself in, as if it were a heavy cloak about someone's shoulders.

Cragfont, one of the South's most unusual architectural and historical treasures, is both commandingly dignified and welcoming, befitting its original builders and occupants, who were courageous but hospitable, the elite of the new nation and yet approachable by one and all.

The origins of Cragfont's longstanding hauntings, which morph and change with the occupants, are not so forthcoming, and the spirits are not eager to disclose their secrets.

It remains one of the most mysterious houses in America.

2

Rosemont

Like the old soldier, we sit by the fireside and talk of comrades of other days; the battles they have fought and victories won. We talk of those now on the field and those who are to come after them. In these discussions, we exhibit the feelings common to man when we maintain that our county, Sumner, has produced, is producing and will continue to produce as good and as many race nags as any county in the United States.
—General Robert Desha

The Glory Days

Unless one knew to look for it, Rosemont would be very easy to pass by, unnoticed, in its location on a main Gallatin artery crowded with run-down businesses in metal buildings, trailer parks and used car lots. But just off the road, on a slight rise, a red-brick Palladian Greek Revival home, with Ionic mammoth white pillars and expansive porches, reclines majestically among enormous trees. This is a home that is almost two hundred years old, and for most of that time, its ownership has remained in one family.

It whispers of happy memories of a lifelong love affair that started when the participants were mere children, playing on the front lawn, while behind the house, prize-winning Thoroughbreds grazed contentedly on the property's five hundred acres. It also holds memories of not-so-good days, when Union soldiers camped on its grounds and its handsome furnishings were taken outside for the army's use. In more recent days, it has seen many weddings in its sumptuous gardens—gardens that are smaller now but were once so esteemed that their design and plantings were copied on estates in Europe.

Jo Conn Guild built his home in late 1836, after returning home from the Seminole War, where he visited New Orleans and admired the architectural style of the elegant homes. He incorporated much of their distinct design into Rosemont, making it unique among Middle Tennessee homes of the early nineteenth century.

The home's construction took over seven years, and during that time, Guild and his wife, Catherine, lived in a small house on the property. Catherine came to believe that one reason it took so long was the workers' reluctance to leave behind her hearty meals she served, and she lamented that it thus took a whole year just to paint the expansive mansion, inside and out.

The home's bricks were fired onsite from clay earth that came from across the street, and the enormous Ionic columns were milled by the enslaved on the property.

Rosemont has been home to generations of children, although during the several pandemics of the 1800s, many did not live to adulthood.

Rosemont is an iconic reminder of the horse farm plantation of the early 1800s in Sumner County, which, at that time, was the Thoroughbred horse breeding and racing center of the South. The red-brick Palladian Greek Revival home with expansive porches was built by lawyer, statesman and turfman Josephus Conn Guild. *Author's collection.*

Self-described "history geek and Civil War reenactor" Eli Geery is the site director at Rosemont. "I actually never wanted anything to do with the idea of spirits and hauntings and that aspect of this historic property," Eli said. "I thought paranormal events had a logical explanation about 99 percent of the time," he went on to say, adding, "until I came to work at Rosemont."

Eli starts his day in his office, formerly the master bedroom of Jo Conn Guild and his wife, Catherine, and later, that of their son Walter, along with his wife, Bettie. "Every morning, at 10:00 a.m., it is as if the family is starting its day," said Eli. "There are vibrations on the floor above me, as if the family is here, walking about." Doors open and close, and some have had to be pinned and tied to keep them open. There are footsteps. "Most notably, there is a recognizable pattern to the footsteps—a loop—that I hear repeatedly every morning from the floor above me, although I am alone in the house."

"It seems to me that the spirits here long for interaction." During paranormal investigations, "we have asked questions, holding a flashlight that is turned off, and they turn it on to signify a 'yes,'" said Eli. "On a daily basis, there is one 'woman' here all the time, and occasionally, a male figure and a child. They seem to be of different generations."

Eli has seen a gentleman walk right in front of him, wearing frumpy clothes; he said he is "translucent, but I could see details of his appearance....I felt a rush of wind as he walked in front of me. He did not acknowledge my presence or seem to know I was there."

A lot goes on at 3:50 a.m. many mornings. The motion sensor will go off inside Eli's locked office.

Walter and Bettie had a son named Walter Jr. who was afflicted with epilepsy, and his bedroom was located next to his parents so that Betty could attend to him in the night if needed, as he suffered periodic losses of speech and headaches. Walter died at nineteen years of age at 3:50 a.m.

> *At Halloween and Christmas, we have LED-lit candles in every window; each one must be turned on by hand, which is a lengthy process, taking about forty minutes—and the same to turn them off in the morning.*
>
> *The lights are known to turn themselves off and on.*
>
> *One morning, we had just turned them all off upstairs, and by the time we got to the bottom of the stairs, they had all been turned on again.*
>
> *My young daughter Lilly was up in the nursery one day, and she came downstairs to tell me there was a man in the nursery but that he had*

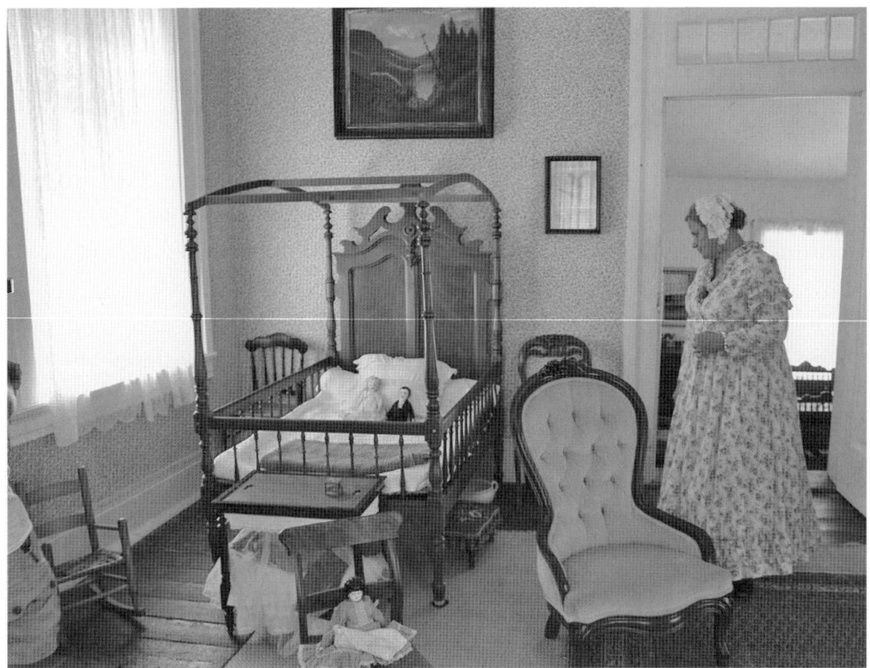

Vonda Dixon, Rose Greenhow's Rear Guard Civil War civilian reenactor, poses in the nursery at Rosemont. Much of the ghostly activity here occurs on the upper story of Rosemont. *Author's collection.*

> *disappeared. She said he was at the fireplace with his arm against the mantel and he "looked at me then disappeared in a blue light."*
>
> *Quite a lot of detail for a seven-year-old to fabricate.*

A little girl on the stairs has been seen by Eli and reported by others. Sadly, deaths among children at Rosemont, as well as throughout the population before modern vaccines, were not unusual. In the first and second generation at Rosemont, nine children died before the age of one.

The upstairs guest bedroom at Rosemont houses brides and their attendants when weddings are held. Once, a group of bridesmaids were crowded into the bathroom next to the guest room, doing their makeup and hair in front of the large mirror over the sink, when suddenly, the water faucet turned on full force, all by itself, without human assistance. "Those of us downstairs heard five pairs of high heels come clattering down the stairs," laughed Eli. "The women wouldn't go back up there."

Rosemont is, quite naturally, a haven for ghost hunters. "Their presence increases the activity in the house every time," said Eli. "At this point, we have more questions than answers, but my theory is that for over one hundred years, Rosemont has entertained politicians, Thoroughbred racing enthusiasts, lawyers, Civil War generals from both sides of the conflict and American icons, such as Sam Houston, Andrew Jackson, Confederate General John Hunt Morgan, and many more," Eli noted. "The spirits, whoever they might be, still have something to say, and they still want to be a part of Rosemont."

~

Jo Conn Guild was born in Virginia in 1802 and came to Sumner County in 1812, but he was soon orphaned and taken in by an uncle. He obtained his law license in 1822 at the age of twenty. Thus began a lifelong devotion to law and politics, as exemplified by his "vigorous representation" of his clients, according to historian Walter T. Durham in *Josephus Conn Guild and Rosemont*. Among his many cases were those protecting the rights of the enslaved and those who had been freed by provisions in their masters' wills but that executors were attempting to subvert. "He left a legacy of courtroom wit and humor without malice…a quintessential advocate of common sense," remarked Durham.

Guild was a "lone wolf" among politically ambitious lawyers when he represented the Cherokee in their plea to remain a sovereign nation, believing that the very earliest treaties proved the country's founders considered them a "distinct entity" that would "bind themselves as a nation." Calling the Natives' removal a blatant "land grab," this was one case that Guild, in all his eloquence and employment of sound legal principles, could not win and it resulted in the Trail of Tears: the relocation of the Cherokee to Oklahoma.

Guild served as both a Tennessee state representative and as a state senator, and his influence was critical in securing public funds for the L&N Railroad line that had its start in Kentucky, ran through Tennessee and ended at the Gulf of Mexico.

A lifelong supporter of his good friend Andrew Jackson, who often stayed at Rosemont, Guild vociferously defended Jackson during Congress's attempt to censure him while he was president.

Guild's passionate interests, aside from the law, were "bearing arms in defense of his country and the breeding and racing of Thoroughbred horses," Durham noted.

The breeding and racing of Thoroughbred horses put Tennessee "on the map," as the leisure class grew in post–Revolutionary War America.

Josephus Conn Guild was a zealous advocate for the legal rights of the enslaved who had inherited their former masters' property. He fought against the removal of Natives from their lands. *Courtesy of the Sumner County Museum.*

The English colonists at Jamestown were those who admired the pasttimes of the British Crown and hoped to create a society in Virginia like the one they had appreciated at home—one in which aristocratic values were strong. At that time in Britain, horse racing was an elite pursuit, aptly named the "sport of kings." The sport would become firmly entrenched in Virginia, but after the American Revolution, the racehorse center of the nation shifted westward and southward. Virginians and Carolinians migrated into Kentucky and Tennessee in the 1700s, and racing and breeding soon flourished in those areas.

"Middle Tennessee had an edge due to its slightly warmer climate, which gave the colts a longer grazing time in the fall. A less-severe winter and earlier grass in the spring gave the area supremacy over Kentucky," said Ridley Wills II.

The first blood horses, as Thoroughbreds were then called, were brought into the Nashville area around 1800. The earliest to arrive may have been Grey Medley, a stallion brought to the farm of William Donelson on the Gallatin Road by Redmond Barry of Gallatin. In 1804, horse racing was inaugurated in Tennessee, at Gallatin. The first day's main event was a race between Andrew Jackson's "Indian Queen" and Doctor Berry's "Polly."

Vonda Dixon is shown in front of Judge Jo Conn Guild's official portrait for the Tennessee Bar Association. The portrait was done from the photograph of Judge Guild in his smoking jacket. Guild used to conduct court in the jacket rather than a traditional judicial robe—a fact deemphasized in his official portrait. *Author's collection.*

Eli Geery is the site director at Rosemont. Here, he is giving a tour of the Thoroughbred farm's elegantly appointed office, located on the lower level of the New Orleans–inspired home. *Author's collection.*

General Robert Desha, of Sumner County, in an article in the *New York Spirit of the Times*, described the prominence of his county in the arena of turf racing on February 8, 1839:

> *As regards that manly and gentlemanly amusement, the sport of the turf... Sumner County, from the earliest period has been and continues to be so much devoted....Like the old soldier, we sit by the fireside and talk of comrades of other days; the battles they have fought and victories won. We talk of those now on the field and those who are to come after them. In these discussions, we exhibit the feelings common to man when we maintain that our county, Sumner, has produced, is producing and will continue to produce as good and as many race nags as any county in the United States.*

"This, I suppose, is the acknowledged centre of the racehorse region," wrote William Giles Harding from Belle Meade to the *American Turf Register* on June 11, 1839. "Blood stock here is all the go. To be without it is to be out of fashion and destitute of taste. So, I, too, have procured a little of the real grit which by-and-by I hope to increase."

During the 1850s, the racing map broadened. The Metairie course in New Orleans became the nation's premier racing center. The components of a fall race's success were a "good crowd, good horses, good accommodations and beautiful ladies....These were the days when men made bets on their judgment of horses and riders not after the postwar fashion of betting on the tips of bookmakers," said Wills in his article "The Eclipse of the Thoroughbred Horse Industry in Tennessee," noting that before the Civil War, Tennessee racecourses and jockey clubs that trained and raced horses were usually owned by local gentlemen with excellent reputations—men such as Guild. This would not be the case after the war.

"The best [horse rubber and attendant] I ever knew was old Isaac Foxhall, Uncle Ike as we familiarly called him, I forbear to call him a slave," said George Guild in the preface to an interview he did with Uncle Ike in the late 1800s to record some of the firsthand memories of the old days in turf racing.

> *I was the first and only child of the family when he came, but I was too young to remember it, and I feel now that he, at once, won my affection and that of the entire family of children. As* [we] *were born and grew up, he was our daily attendant. As the years wore on, he became my father's chief attendant for the care of the blooded horses, feeding, rubbing and breeding the mares and looking after their foals.*

When colts were prepared for the races, Guild generally placed them in the hands of a White trainer, but Uncle Ike served as the head rubber and attendant and took judicious care of the horses when they were taken to the track. Consequently, Uncle Ike knew all of the great racecourses in the South, including those in Savannah, New Orleans and Memphis.

Races were typically held twice a year—in summer and fall—with elaborate house parties and guests coming from all over the South and even points north to enjoy the camaraderie and festive atmosphere surrounding the matches. "Great numbers of the first ladies of the land would attend the races," wrote Walter Durham. "They were given the best seats in the grandstand, and a number of gentlemen were always detailed to wait upon them and look after their comfort and enjoyment of the sport."

Uncle Ike's musings, as told to George Guild, give a colorful account of the flavor and celebratory atmosphere of a race in the 1850s in New Orleans, in which a Guild racehorse, Beeswing, was running.

> *When Thursday came in, when the horn blows at 12:00 o'clock for the horses to come out that we're going to run, I went out, leading Beeswing by the bit.*
>
> *I had her looking fine and her mane platted up with blue ribbons and her coat rubbed 'till you would see your face in her, like a looking glass.*
>
> *Marse Jo and Mr. Watson was walking in front, and Tom Hall, who was to ride her in the race, was just behind and all dressed up in new riding clothes: white pants with red stripes down the side, a red jacket in his hand.*
>
> *Along with him was two of the stable boys, carrying Beeswing's training clothes and some blankets to throw over her when she run a heat. Just before we passed, I pulled out the sheet that I had put on her. The people, and especially de ladies, could see the prettiest race mare ever was trained. I never heard such shouting as we passed by in my born days, especially from the ladies who liked never stopped hollering for Beeswing.*
>
> *Gentlemens, I never felt so proud in my life.*
>
> *There was more people on the track dere to seed that race than I ever expect to see anywhere on this earth.*
>
> *This was at New Orleans.*

The Devastation of War

The Civil War devastated the stud farms and racecourses of Confederate Tennessee. Racetracks were closed and torn up, and valuable Thoroughbreds were volunteered by willing patriots for Confederate use or later seized for use as cavalry horses by the occupying forces of the Union.

Kentucky did not secede and was able to continue racing in Lexington throughout the war, leading to the most profitable races shifting from Tennessee to Kentucky, with the highest purses and Thoroughbreds without peer. The Kentucky-Tennessee Thoroughbred rivalry would veer back and forth between the two states for many years; however, Tennessee never fully recovered from the war's devastation of its finest stock and farms.

The Civil War saw Guild commit to the preservation of the Union, with one caveat: the government held its powers by consent of the governed, and that consent was not being felt in the South. This belief set him at odds with one of his closest Sumner County friends, Bailie Peyton, his brother turfman and horse breeder, and with Andrew Johnson, a two-term Tennessee governor. Johnson would later attempt to make an example of Guild by ordering his arrest for "treasonable language" and "using his influence against the government of the United States." Guild was imprisoned in Nashville and then taken to Fort Mackinac in the northernmost area of Michigan, along with two prominent Nashvillians.

Durham wrote that the affable and elegant Guild and his friends charmed all sorts of people along the way to prison, enjoying good meals and fine company, but encountered a "wild and crawfishy looking lot" in Michigan who were determined to do harm to the "Rebels."

In Michigan, Guild was permitted to observe the trial of a Native accused of murder. Guild thought the Native's attorney was doing a substandard job, as there was clearly a case for self-defense. Guild was generously allowed to assume the position of the defense lawyer for the man, and he was subsequently acquitted.

All of this occurred in the space of less than a year before Guild and his companions were allowed to return home. In the interview with Uncle Ike, George Guild got the horseman's point of view of an incident at Rosemont while Jo Guild was incarcerated at Fort Mackinac:

> *Well, I tell you the first them folks at the North done was they sended Andy Johnson down here to be military governor. I know him well, for he was a great friend of Marse Jo, and when Andy Johnson was speaking around, wanting office, he always come to our house and stay all night.*
>
> *Well, sirs, the first thing he done on getting at the capitol, he sent his soldiers around and arrested Marse Jo and three of his best friends and sent them off way up north and put him in jail close. I tell you how Marse Joe got out of that jail in der North.*
>
> *Mr. John Morgan* [General John Hunt Morgan, Confederate army] *with his soldiers come to Gallatin an capture one thousand Yankee soldiers that were here at the Sumner County fairground, and when he was here, Mr. John Morgan come out to our house to see Ole Miss and the girls, an' Ole Miss told him how Mr. Andy Johnson had treated Marse Jo for his friendship.*

The dining room table, when all leaves are inserted, seats twenty-four people. It was a wedding gift to the Guilds and was made locally. The stains and gouges are "a snapshot of what occurred at so many fine homes in the area during the Civil War," says Eli Geery. "Here, we see ink stains from a blotter used by Union commanders to write dispatches to the field, as well as knife marks and burns" from careless use. *Author's collection.*

> *Mr. Morgan say, "Don't you be uneasy, I'll fix that up in a few days," and he did do it sho enough, and I'll tell you how: he just take a part of his men with him an went up to Kentucky an captured a judge just like Marse Jo is, and when they hear of it in Washington, they swapped one judge for the other, and Marse Jo he came home after he had been in the North for about one whole year, and he like to froze to death up there, for it was winter de most of the time.*
>
> *Mr. Brownlow was governor down at Nashville, and I tell you, all said they were the cruelest men they could have put over our White folks. It would take me a month or more to tell you one half a what they done in them four years' war.*

At one point in the Civil War, the Union army camped on Rosemont's grounds and used the house and its furnishings at will. Horses were appropriated, and furniture was taken out on the lawn, which Guild's wife bore with dignity, said Eli Geery, "until they took her dining room table outside" and treated it brutally with ink, coffee and knives. "This was the last

Susan King stands beside a silver service belonging to the Guilds that was hidden beneath the floorboards of the house to keep it safe during the Civil War. Servants were able to store a majority of the Guilds' valuables under the house during the Union occupation of their house and grounds. *Author's collection.*

straw, and all five-foot-tall of religious fervency and indignation in the form of Mrs. Guild was unleashed upon the Yankees, who promptly returned the table to the dining room." The house was the "province of the women," said Eli. "Men spent most of their time out in the field or in the barns; the women pretty much ran the house," Eli explained.

"Mrs. Guild was staunchly religious and did not condone gambling," said Eli, although she certainly benefitted from the winnings and accepted the silver trophies and mementoes of racing into Rosemont. "What she didn't see or have firsthand knowledge of never happened," laughed Eli. This would not have been unusual for the time. The exorbitant betting and rough-and-tumble atmosphere surrounding the buying, selling, breeding, training and maintenance of these horses were part of a man's world in the antebellum South and not meant for females.

Men gathered in the semidetached office of Judge Guild to conduct "horse" business and frequented the barns and outbuildings associated with the Thoroughbreds.

There have been two full-bodied apparitions seen in the window of the judge's office, but their identities are unknown.

Changing Times, Changing Fortunes

The post–Civil War era never saw the return of the glory days of horse farms and racing in Tennessee.

George Guild wrote of the waning years of turf racing:

> *Racing is not now as it was then. As I have said, the first men of the land were lovers of the turf, and it was on a high plane. Nothing but gentlemen could become members of the racing club, and a breach of honesty and integrity of principle in racing would occasion at once an expulsion with an order no more for the individual to participate in the sport or to make an entry for a stake. Blood and ability to repeat was then in these olden times the only evidence of the racehorse in thoroughbred.*
>
> *The races later became for speed alone, which, according to the old turf racers, is no test of a racehorse. Gamblers make money by unfair means. They lack what makes gentlemen of the character of former times when engaged in this sport; not lovers of the high Thoroughbred but for the money that is in it by unfair and disgraceful means to be attained.*

The excitement of bringing home silver trophies won on prominent racecourses, the days of elegant parties in honor of the racing season and the gossip and animated talk on the track and in the viewing stands were all gone, as fortunes and the times had changed.

Walter Guild, the son of the judge, was the judge's favorite. At the age of five, he and little Bettie Alexander would play on the front lawn of Rosemont, and at that young age, they vowed to marry each other when they grew up. The two were very different: Walter was quiet and thoughtful; Bettie, when "of age," became one of the most popular young belles in Sumner County and was enthusiastically welcomed at every social gathering. "Walter was not a 'joiner' like the rest of the family; he was no politician, although people tended to listen to his advice," said Eli

The Civil War history of Rosemont is portrayed in living history presentations throughout the year on the grounds of Rosemont. Here, reenactors portraying Confederate soldiers drill in preparation for battle. *Courtesy of Eli Geery.*

Geery. Walter was quite possibly dyslexic, as his writings show a tendency to reverse letters. As a result, he did not attend the boarding schools and prestigious institutes of higher learning that the other Guild offspring did, but he completed college, nevertheless. Bettie was outgoing and fiery and could cuss like a man, despite her gentility.

Although Walter was seriously wounded in the Civil War and spent the remainder of his years often bedridden or in a semicoma for weeks at a time, heavily sedated with the opiates of the day, the couple had nine children. "We know that after the war, though still in his twenties, Walter didn't go back upstairs again, or if he did, it was rare," said Eli. Walter could sit up in the bed and, from the window, watch the Confederate veteran reunions and other gatherings, some with two thousand participants, on the same lawn on which he had proposed to Bettie at the age of five, although he was too crippled to attend.

Rosemont was a gathering place during its first 150 years, and it is still a gathering place for weddings, receptions, club meetings, ghost hunts and living history reenactments.

In 1923 Bettie Guild lay dying in the same bed in which Walter had spent so many long, pain-filled days, her family and housekeeping staff around her. As her death neared, an owl flew down the chimney, lit on the hearth and then came to rest on one post of her four-poster bed. The owl remained there until Bettie took her last breath, then flew back up the chimney. Family lore says the owl was Walter, saying goodbye.

Epilogue and Author's Notes

By the mid-1840s, Judge Josephus Conn Guild's political gatherings at Rosemont had grown in frequency and in size. The card games, occasional swearing and alcohol that gentlemen naturally favored when discussing the tumultuous affairs of the day were becoming intrusive into Guild's wife's genteel home.

Using leftover bricks from the construction of Rosemont, Guild constructed a two-room structure on the eastern edge of Gallatin, at the end of Franklin Street. Guild believed the leftover bricks were the rejects that were not of the quality he wanted in the construction of Rosemont, so he had plaster applied over them to strengthen them. The house was nicknamed the "Plaster House." This was a meeting hall for men after their workday was done, a "man cave" of sorts for the movers and shakers of young Sumner County.

The Plaster House was Judge Guild's meeting place until the Union army took it over for use as a hospital. In recent years, it has served a succession of businesses, including renowned artist Ralph McDonald's gallery and

Judge Guild used leftover bricks from the construction of Rosemont to construct the Plaster House on College Street, just half a block from where Guild's law office was located. The two-room structure was a gathering place for the political meetings of the day. *Author's collection.*

production facility for his wildlife prints and giclées that are printed and shipped around the world.

The author of this book has lived next door to the Plaster House for twenty years. She has seen lights go off and on late at night and what appeared to be glowing, lit cigars held by unseen hands and has heard horse hooves walking on the gravel driveway of the property. She has smelled whiskey wafting on a breeze in the vicinity of the Plaster House's back door. Legend says John Hunt Morgan rode his horse through the open back door and out the opposite open front door one hot summer night early on in the Civil War.

While walking her dog past the property, the author has observed a full-bodied apparition of a Union soldier, clad in an officer's uniform, his hands clasped behind his back, smoking a cigar and looking up at the sky. Her dog would not go to the spot where the man was seen, even after the apparition vanished.

Once, while conducting the Gallatin Ghost Walk History and Mystery tour, the author was standing on the front porch of the Plaster House when she noticed that the foyer lights had not been turned on, as they usually are

During recent renovations at the Plaster House, Judge Guild's political meeting headquarters on College Street in Gallatin, a horse's head suddenly appeared overnight as a chunk out of the plaster, a reminder of the original owner's passion for the turf and his place in Thoroughbred history. Workers on-site firmly deny having any part in the head's appearance. It is just one of the many paranormal occurrences at this historic home that was used as a hospital during the Civil War. *Author's collection.*

so that ghost walk attendees can better see the ornamental cranberry glass insets around the front door. As the tour walked away, the author said to the group, "I wish the lights had been on so we could have seen the beautiful glass glow." At that moment, the lights came on.

A benign spirit seems to inhabit the property, and some former occupants of the Plaster House have said that although they see fleeting shadows in the halls and, occasionally, objects move about, they really have never felt fear; rather, they feel protected. The author tends to believe the presence at Plaster House is Judge Guild spending some of his afterlife hours where he shared so many spirited and enlightened political discussions and convivial hours with dear friends.

3

The Most Haunted Public Square in America

It was a good day today in Gallatin. No one was hanged.
—Alice Williamson diary

By 1850, the original land grant farms of Middle Tennessee were prosperous plantation-based agricultural and horse farms, the latter breeding, raising and training some of the most valuable Thoroughbred horses in the country. National reputations and fortunes were resplendent in the more than one hundred showplace homes—not only those of General Winchester at Cragfont but also those of Josephus Conn Guild at Rosemont, Daniel Smith Donelson at Hazel Path and Isaac Franklin at Fairvue.

Thirty communities were served by a stagecoach line, river trade and ferry services, and in the mid-1850s, the construction of the L&N Railroad from Louisville to Nashville would make Sumner County a hub of commerce and manufacturing, particularly known for its distilleries and mills.

Two newspapers, several doctors and dentists and many attorneys served the area. The volume of litigation in the courts of the county not only sustained the lawyers but also contributed to the successful operation of several hotels and boardinghouses to accommodate litigants' lengthy stays for court proceedings.

Tennessee is second only to Virginia in its number of Civil War battles that occurred in the state, yet Sumner County saw no heavy action during the four years of the conflict. Instead, it endured three torturous years of chaos, uncertainty, brutality and devastation, largely due to the excessive and heavy-handed actions of Union general Eleazer Paine, the commander of occupying troops from late 1862 until early 1864.

The county sent 3,200 troops to the Confederate effort, and by the time of Paine's arrival in Gallatin, Sumner Countians had suffered the loss of husbands, brothers and sons in significant battles, such as those at Shiloh and Fort Donelson—defeats that left the entirety of Middle Tennessee in enemy hands.

America's Civil War had not even been in existence two years when a *New York Times* reporter accompanying the Union army as it marched across the South filed regular missives for publication to a northern audience that appreciated his sarcasm and derision of conditions in *Davisiana*, a term he used for the Confederate States of America, under their president, Jefferson Davis. In November 1862, he visited Middle Tennessee and wrote a story for the paper and identified himself only as "Our Correspondent." Though he mocked the despondent and grieving population of Gallatin, Tennessee, the county seat of Sumner County, his writings accurately depicted the bleak and somber conditions.

Only very old men, young children and women were left in the once-prosperous town, and most of those who remained were in mourning for loved ones killed in battle. Concurrent with the Union army's invasion of Sumner, the local government, schools and many churches ceased to function. Newspapers and businesses were closed, and individual teachers conducted classes in their own homes. During the war years, there was a general absence of public records in Sumner County.

On November 24, 1862, the writer filed this report:

> *This place was reached yesterday, and the army went into temporary encampment. Gallatin is the county seat of Sumner County and contains about three thousand inhabitants, who are as rebellious as any in all Davisiana could wish.*
>
> *The people along our route through the county looked as though they would, if they had the power, hurl us to the regions of Pluto. Not a Union flag was anywhere seen, not a sign of welcome was exhibited, and not a word of cheer greeted us at any point.*

Brigadier General John Hunt Morgan, CSA. *Courtesy of the Library of Congress.*

> *As the column passed through Gallatin, the women looked upon us either with the contempt of the veriest vixens or with the solemnity of those who are viewing the funeral procession of their dearest friends. Occasionally,* [a] *saucy young she-rebel would venture to an upper window and condescend to look at us, but as soon as she saw that she was attracting our notice, she withdrew with a contemptuous toss of the head.*
>
> *Sumner County is thoroughly rebellious. She has furnished more troops for the rebel service than any county in the state, according to her population. There are very few young men in the state; they have nearly all gone into the rebel army; the female portion of the population is intensely rebel.*
>
> *Most of the women you meet, both young and old, are dressed in black, worn for the loss of some near relative who has died or been killed in the rebel service. Gallatin has been famous as the point of Morgan's most successful raids upon the Louisville and Nashville Railroad, which runs immediately through the place. This is the point where Gen. R.W. Johnson, with his command and a large quantity of government stores, were captured in August last by Morgan and his band. From* [Hartsville,] *Tennessee, Morgan has been accustomed to lead his men to this place, attack the trains, destroy our* [supplies] *and return to the mountains almost without impunity. The citizens of this section regard Morgan as some ubiquitous demigod, possessing all the qualities of manliness and chivalry, as well as a charmed life against the steel and bullets of the Union forces.*

Indeed, the name Morgan struck fear in the heart of any Union soldier or commander and adulation in the beating breasts of southern rebels. The flamboyant, charismatic and cunning general had reached a mythic stature with his raids on Union supplies. He might strike a Union train one day and cause chaos in an occupied town the next; liberate supplies from a Yankee warehouse, then turn and sabotage an entire stretch of railroad track by twisting its rails into what became known as "Morgan's neckties."

Again, the *New York Times*, on November 24, 1862, said:

> *There is, it is said, but one true Union man in Gallatin.*
>
> *There is here an extensive manufactory of coarse cotton goods, which did an immense business in the service of the rebels last year....There have been no schools in session for some time. The country in which we are is beautiful, fertile, and comparatively well improved, yet on all sides, the withering, blighting effects of the rebellion are visible. Uncultivated fields, dilapidated outhouses, vacant residences, empty schoolhouses, wasted farmland, and neglected children show the pestilential effects of treason that has carried everything before it.*
>
> *It will be some days before the railroad tunnel is repaired though the work will be prosecuted as fast as possible. The entire tunnel has been blown in* [by Morgan, just days before. His actions stopped the movement of Union supplies south for over ninety days].

Gallatin loved General Morgan.

Confederate general Basil Duke, Morgan's brother-in-law and comrade in arms, accompanied him on his raids through Middle Tennessee and commented in his memoirs on the reverence and affection the Gallatin citizenry held for Morgan, telling of the local ladies' generous baking of sweets and "dainties" to show their love of the troops, though their pantries were meager due to the privations of war.

The admiration was mutual.

> *It will be impossible for the men, whose history I am writing, to ever forget this period of their lives. The beautiful country in which it was passed, the blue grass pastures and the noble trees, the encampments in the shady forests, through which ran the clear cool Tennessee waters, the lazy enjoyments of the green bivouacs, changing abruptly to the excitement of the chase and the action, the midnight moonlit rides amidst the lovely scenery, cause the recollections which crowd our minds, when we think of Gallatin and Hartsville, to mingle almost inseparably with the descriptions of romance.*
>
> *In this country live a people worthy of it. In all the qualities which win respect and love, in generosity, honesty, devoted friendship, zealous adherence to what they deem the right, unflinching support of those who labor for it, in hospitality and kindliness, the creator never made a people to excel them.*

In one maneuver that exemplifies the daring and brash conduct that he applied against the enemy, Morgan and his men rode into Gallatin disguised as federal officers. They went to the telegraph office, commandeered by a Union man, and cunningly extracted military intelligence through flattery and sheer hubris. The telegraph operator couldn't resist bragging a bit about what his own actions would be should he encounter the devil, Morgan. Morgan then ended the charade. He put out his hand and said, "Give me that pistol….I am Morgan."

The depredations of Morgan to the vital railroad lines charged with moving Union supplies to battles in the deeper South resulted in the appointment of a controversial figure as commanding general of occupied Gallatin: General Eleazer Paine.

Eleazer A. Paine was born on September 10, 1815, in Ohio and attended West Point, graduating in 1839. Paine was appointed second lieutenant in the First U.S. Infantry and served for a year in the Florida War against the Seminoles before resigning in 1840. Despite his limited military experience, in 1843, he wrote and published a training manual titled *Military Instructions; Designed for the Militia and Volunteers.*

Paine returned to Ohio and studied law, passing the bar in 1843 and becoming a lawyer in Painesville, Ohio, a town named for his ancestor. In 1848, he moved farther west to Monmouth, Illinois, where he married and raised a family. One of Paine's close friends was fellow Illinois attorney Abraham Lincoln. Rising in the Union command at the Civil War's beginnings, Paine quickly established a reputation as a "'hanging general' [and] was a controversial figure….[He was] severely criticized [by his own command] for an order issued in Cairo, Illinois, in response to a report that five Union men had been murdered by Rebel cavalry near Bloomfield, Missouri, on February 8, 1862, and Paine had ordered his troops in Missouri to 'Hang one of the rebel cavalry for each Union man murdered, and after this, two for each. Continue to scout, capture, and kill,'" wrote Walter Durham in *Rebellion Revisited.*

Paine was put in charge of a brigade stationed at Paducah and ordered by General Grant not to offend the citizens of Paducah, even though they might be southern sympathizers. General Paine ignored these orders. He said that he "was compelled to be severe, for nearly every man is a rank secessionist," and he had several southern sympathizers exiled to Canada and some Confederate prisoners executed. Grant wrote that General Paine was "entirely unfit to command a post." After ninety days, he was reassigned at the request of the governor of Kentucky.

But political connections and an abject fear of John Hunt Morgan after the tunnel was blown up made Paine the perfect occupying commander for

Brigadier General Eleazar Paine, a colonel of the Ninth Illinois Infantry. *Courtesy of the Library of Congress.*

a highly rebellious Sumner County, despite his despotic temperament and penchant for overkill. Under Paine's command, martial law, defined in Black's law dictionary as "a system of law, pertaining only in time of actual war and growing out of the exigencies thereof, arbitrary in its character, and depending only on the will of its commander…suspends all existing civil laws, as well as the civil authority and the ordinary administration of justice," assumed an especially brutal nature.

Alice Williamson was a sixteen-year-old girl in Gallatin at the time of the occupation. One of the most trenchant but telling entries in her diary about life under Paine is the simple statement, "It was a good day today in Gallatin. No one was hanged."

The occupying army in Gallatin had two assignments: protect the rail and water lines and police the civilian population. In 1862, they built Fort Thomas just north of the railroad line in the city. In addition, one of Paine's first accomplishments was to appropriate virtually every suitable church or public building for use as a hospital. Because records of the time are scarce, the conservative estimate is that eight to ten of these hospitals were quickly put forth, but there were countless private homes that housed soldiers from both sides of the conflict who were brought by rail to Gallatin.

In 1863, General Paine tightened the military's control over the Gallatin area. The entire region had seen many of its best and brightest killed in battle, leaving widows and orphans with little means to support themselves and rendering the formerly lush and productive fields withered and desolate. The formerly quiet and rural county seat of Gallatin was then filled with the chaos and uncertainty of a conquered populace occupied by a brutal dictator with a sadistic streak.

Paine was known not only for executing suspected rebel spies without a trial but also his decidedly warped executions involving setting prisoners free on old horses and then chasing them down with Union soldiers on good mounts. It was a "game" devised by Paine known as "chasing the fox with fresh horses," as Williamson reported in her diary.

Soldiers on leave who attempted to return home to visit loved ones risked torture and death at the orders of General Paine.

Paine also had a fondness for scouting the loveliest homes in the countryside and taking furniture and other valuables for his own use.

The following are some entries from Alice's diary, wherein she refers to Paine by numerous "pet" names:

> *March 12th* [1864]
> *Old Payne* [sic] *dined at Mrs. Hales today: everyone despises him but are afraid to show it. Yesterday, he went up the country a few miles to a Mr. Dalton's whose son came home from the southern army the day before and had the same day taken the amnesty oath.*
>
> *Riding up to the door, he enquired of Mr. Dalton if his son was at home, but before he answered, his son came to the door.*
>
> *Old Nick then told him to get his horse and go with him.*
>
> *After insulting the father, he carried his son a half mile away and shot him six times.*
>
> *One of Payne's* [sic] *escorts, hearing the young man groan with pain, placed a pistol to his temple and remarked, "I will stop that, sir," he shot him again.*
>
> *But this is nothing new; this is the fifth man that has been shot in this way, besides numbers that have been carried off by scouts and never return.*
>
> *March 12th*
> *I learn today that Gen. Payne* [sic] *had no charge against Mr. Dalton, so he told his* [Dalton's] *father. After killing him, he rode back to the house and told Mr. D. that his son was in sight—he could bury him if he wished.*
>
> *Today, a gentleman (Col. E____) was in Payne's* [sic] *office when he was trying a young man about sixteen years old, and the only support of an aged father who was with him. His crime was being a rebel. Payne* [sic] *sent the young man to jail, telling the guard to bring him out at seven o'clock.*
>
> *The father actually fell upon his knees before the heartless tyrant but was heartlessly bidden to rise and go home, the young man has never been heard of since.*
>
> *March 12th*
> *Weather moderate; so is old Payne* [sic], *but as weather is changeable, our general is, too.*

March 16th
Pleasant weather cannot last always, and as old hurricane changes with the weather, a rainy day bodes no good for us. Today, a scout was sent out under Capt. Payne [sic] *(son of Tempest) and a man with him a stranger. Everyone knows his fate; and many were the prayers that ascended to heaven for his sake.*

March 22nd
Cold and windy. Paynes [sic] *behavior moderate. No murdering going on. Grand military ball coming off Tuesday 29th.*

The "only Union man in Sumner County," Bailie Peyton, a statesman and Thoroughbred horse farmer, relentlessly appealed to his friend Abraham Lincoln to remove Paine from Gallatin, according to Walter Durham in *Rebellion Revisited.*

Paine was removed from the post on April 29, 1864, by the orders of Major General William T. Sherman.

Gallatin resident Jerry Lumpkins is a retired schoolteacher, author and historian. In 2012, he portrayed Eleazer Paine in the Gallatin City Cemetery Tour "after several other people turned the role down," laughed Lumpkins. "They just didn't want their reputation sullied by being associated with the most hated man ever to live in Sumner County," said Lumpkins.

Jerry Lumpkins agreed to portray Union General Eleazar Paine, "the most hated man ever to grace Sumner County," during a Gallatin City Cemetery Tour. *Author's collection.*

"*Greedy, narcissistic, paranoid*: these are all words I would use to describe Paine, based on his reign of terror in Gallatin," said Lumpkins. "There is no telling the actual number of young men from Sumner County that Paine executed," said Lumpkins. Estimates range from 90 to 130. "Southern sympathizers permeated the county," he went on to say. "And everyone was under suspicion, especially young men who might be either in the southern army or coming to the South's aid….He executed people at will; he took their cattle and their horses for the Union cause," said Lumpkins, "and for himself....It is not unusual to read accounts of Paine riding out into the countryside, going into the fine homes of Sumner County and taking anything he wanted in terms of personal belongings: jewelry, silver, paintings; he is reputed to have shipped train cars full of valuables back to his home in Illinois."

Lumpkins said he used the character of Paine in the tour "not so much to give Paine a voice in Gallatin's history but to show the conflicts and triumph of the Gallatin people" during the tragic and devastating occupation years.

SPECTRE FROM THE PAST

Encountering General Eleazer Paine would have been frightening enough in 1862, but to see him 160 years later is both terrifying and impossible.

Wanette Turner, her husband, Jeff, and their son lived in a loft on the Gallatin Public Square for several years, beginning in 2012. Their apartment overlooks the exact spot where Paine hanged so many innocent civilians. "Our first Christmas there, we put up a nine-foot-tall Christmas tree because it would fit in the living room's twelve-foot-tall ceilings," said Wanette Turner. "When we were taking it down and my husband was trying to get it all back in the box, he glanced up and saw a man, a transparent apparition, standing there looking at him." Jeff interjected, "I could tell he was a high-ranking military person because of his bearing and his uniform, and he looked, well, arrogant....He didn't say anything and just looked at me with piercing eyes full of curiosity," said Jeff. "You could tell he was used to giving orders and having them followed. I thought he had a hat on his head, but I am not sure about that."

"During that same time frame, our bedroom faced the square, and one evening, while we were sleeping, I awoke to the sounds of infantry marching and signaling to stop and go—like a soldiers' brigade walking though the square. I got up, and there was nothing there. I went back to bed and heard it again; and again, nothing was there," said Jeff.

Jeff was shown a photograph of General Eleazer Paine, and it did not take him more than a second to exclaim, "That's him! That's the man that watched me put away the Christmas tree." Then, a shaken Wanette revealed, "And that's the same man I saw at the foot of my bed one night, just staring at me. Then he disappeared."

The Nineteenth Ohio Volunteer Infantry drilling on the Gallatin Public Square, 1862. *Courtesy of the Tennessee State Library and Archives, www.tnsos.org.*

But the appearance of Paine was not the only paranormal experience the family had during their stay on the square. "We heard that a brothel used to be next door. The former owner told us she was working in the store one day, and a little boy came running across the show room floor and was dressed in little knee pants—early 1900s attire," said Wanette. "The common wall we shared used to have an undertaker on the other side over one hundred years ago. The entrance of our apartment from the sidewalk, in an old photo, shows a sign designating 'undertaker.' We often heard creaking and odd sounds at the strangest times."

Wanette and the Turners' young son experienced a very frightening event late one night. "In the alley behind the apartment, we heard growling, like a wolf. I kept talking and trying to ignore it to not frighten my son, but as it turned out, he interrupted me after I heard it more than once and said, 'You're not going to tell me you didn't hear that. Look and see if it is a dog.'" Wanette said, "I did get up and look. It was not a dog. It was demonic. I prayed over the space, and we never heard from it again."

Hangman's Noose

Residents in other apartments located above businesses on the square report problems with ghosts, the paranormal and unexplained occurrences.

Whitney Kenney said she got used to making dinner, "putting it on plates on the counter, turning my back, then finding the plates had moved somewhere else on the counter from where they were just put." Whitney lived on the west side of the square. When she and her boyfriend first moved in, "we installed a towel rack and a dry erase board, and both would crash to the floor," no matter how many times they were screwed into the wall. "We've heard voices and conversations in the hallway when we are certain we are the only ones in the entire building."

"One day, Michael went to take the trash out to the curb, and when he came back, he couldn't open the door. It wasn't locked, it simply couldn't be opened; eventually, he had to break it down, but in the meantime, I was going around the frame with a knife from the inside, and he was going around the outside with a screwdriver, to no avail. It was like it was nailed or sealed shut," Whitney said. "I was in, and he was out," Whitney remembered, "and it was very scary. What if there was a fire, and we couldn't get out?" The couple had two children, and they were worried about a fire breaking out or another emergency and not being able to get in—or out.

Then there was the incident of the painted bed. "My five-year-old daughter wanted a wooden bed painted pink, so we got a solid oak bed from a friend and took it completely apart and painted all the pieces. It was in pieces all over the living room, so we left it to dry overnight. Michael and I were all alone, so we know no one could have done to the bed what we saw done to it when we woke up." Stick figures were drawn on the painted bed, and they were "Scary faces…even though they were primitive stick drawings, they had Xs for eyes and straight-stick-crooked frowny-face mouths…and *nooses around their necks*," Whitney shivered. "We sanded again and painted again…three times. The faces came back. We gave up. We put an owl applique sticker over the faces."

But this was not the only time the stick figure with a noose was seen. "Once, we opened our A/C closet in the hall, and a stick figure, just like the one drawn on the bed, had been drawn on the inside of the door, high up."

The couple moved from the apartment, and they took the painted bed with them. But when their child had outgrown it, they didn't take it to Goodwill or put it on the curb for someone to scavenge. "I don't want anyone to have that bed. It just needed to be destroyed. So, we did."

Were the stick figures with nooses a message from spirits regarding the over one hundred innocent civilians hanged on the square during the Union occupation?

The courthouse on the square was occupied by Paine and his attendant officers conducting day-to-day operations, such as issuing passes to those citizens whom they judged to be trustworthy to leave the confines of the city for a few hours and granting privileges to those who took the oath of allegiance to the United States. They also conducted trials for citizens accused of crimes against the Union. Most of the charges were fabricated and meant as a show of force against the populace. The "trial" often took place one day and the hanging was carried out the next day. A mere twenty-five feet from the courthouse stood the gallows, at the ready.

Phantom Fires and Timeslips

There are many dark afternoons in a Sumner County winter, when the sun sets before 5:00 p.m. and businesses and stores lock their doors in the vicinity of the Gallatin Public Square, including the municipal offices and those of the county courts. Often, there will be a smell in the air that is unmistakably that of burning wood and, more particularly, that of a campfire. A campfire has a distinctive smell, and it differs depending on the wood being consumed.

One night in the mid-1960s, two young boys were walking down Franklin Street, headed for the bustling activity of the square, specifically that of the Palace Theater, to see the latest shoot-'em-up Western movie. It was dark, and they hurried past Miss Betsy Boyers' Dance Academy, which was rumored to be haunted.

Suddenly, a fire appeared before them, and as they got closer, they saw that it was a campfire and that men in blue uniforms were seated around it. As they closed in on the scene, the men and the fire vanished into thin air.

We can speculate that this is one of many "timeslips" that occur in Sumner County—occasions when the "now" is eclipsed by something in the past, as real as if it were currently happening.

What the boys saw was a scene that is replicated around the county from time to time. They are windows to the past, when Union soldiers were camped in many a field and by many a stream of water, on farms and on expansive grounds of horse plantations.

Haunted Surgery

During the Civil War, there were no fewer than nine hospitals in the immediate vicinity of the public square, making the atmosphere on any

Andrew Jackson trading card. *Author's collection.*

given day in the central city one of bustling activity. The wounded were brought in on carts from the railroad tracks. Facing the courthouse, on the side of the public square with the gallows, was a Civil War surgery, where the worst of the wounded were treated—but seldom walked out alive.

Attorney Bryan Roehrig has been practicing bankruptcy law in Gallatin since the 1980s in a building on the public square that was reputed to be the law office of Andrew Jackson when he served as a circuit travelling district attorney in the late 1700s. The brick structure, which sits on the east side of the square in a row of buildings dominated by attorneys' offices, is reputedly the most haunted on the square, but "the hauntings, as I have experienced them, have absolutely nothing to do with Old Hickory," Roehrig asserted.

Andrew Jackson's illustrious career and his legendary presence in American history began in 1788, when he came to what is now Tennessee and was sworn in as a lawyer.

The federal government was, at that time, headquartered in Philadelphia. In 1789, Congress created a judicial district for the territory encompassing what is now the Nashville area, and a young Andrew Jackson was appointed to the post of district attorney. "The judicial system was crude, and cases were tried in what corresponded to the county court after the state government was formed," wrote Arthur Colyer in *The Life and Times of Andrew Jackson.*

> *Criminal cases, and perhaps others, were tried by juries. Jackson had two courts in what was then called West Tennessee, one at Nashville and one at Gallatin, besides one at Jonesboro, one at Greenville and one at Knoxville.*
>
> *There is a well-established incident in the life of Jackson during the first years of his terms as attorney general.... The facts were first given me by Judge Jo Conn Guild, who said that when he came to the bar at Gallatin—which must have been as early as 1825—there was an old court record in the county court clerk's office, an entry, the date being shortly after Jackson entered upon the duties of his office in about these words: "The court thanks Andrew Jackson for his brave conduct."*

Curious to know something more about the entry, [Guild] *heard of two old men who were still living who had been members of the county court at the time Jackson was attorney general; he hunted them up and asked them what the entry meant…they gave him this account:*

"That there was a gang of bullies in the county, who, on public days, got up fights and committed other offenses and then bullied the court and refused to be tried; that up to the time Jackson went there as attorney general, the justices holding the court had been dominated by these bullies; that Jackson had full information before he came of the condition; that he came on horseback, hitched his horse and came into court, which had already been opened, and getting his docket out looked over the cases, and the first thing he did was to call one of the cases in which the defendants had refused to be tried; that the defendant came up and said he was not going to be tried.

"Judge Guild's remembrance was that the old men who had been on the bench at the time said that Jackson, in a mild way, remonstrated with the man about his case, and told him that the case had to be tried; that as an officer he was obliged to try it, that the defendant used offensive language and said no court could try him, that thereupon Jackson pulled his saddlebags out from under the table and took out two large pistols—such as travelers carried—and laid them on the table. The bully grabbed at the pistols, and the struggle between him and Jackson led to a general fight.

"The good citizens [of Gallatin], *being inspired by the courage of young Jackson, fell in and whipped out the whole crowd, Jackson and his man, having fallen out the door, Jackson held to him and brought him back and tried him, and when it was all over, the court ordered the clerk to put on the minutes what Judge Guild assured me he had seen: 'The Court thanks Andrew Jackson for his brave conduct.'"*

I have now before me Judge Guild's Parton's Life of Andrew Jackson, *and on the margin of pages 136–137 of the first volume, in Judge Guild's handwriting, is a pencil memorandum showing the facts in brief—in substance, as I have here stated them—and especially giving the words of the order of the minutes. Judge Guild always maintained that in the early days, a fighting lawyer was highly appreciated by his clients and that this exhibition at Gallatin had much to do in giving Jackson the large* [collections] *business that he had. From all the evidence that can be gathered up and from reports that came down to the old men of the present generation, Jackson was a most vigilant prosecuting officer. A good many of his indictments have been gathered up, and they are good common law indictments.*

Jackson's years in Gallatin encompassed the late 1700s and very early 1800s, and he was a frequent guest in several of the most prominent homes of the county, even after he moved on to other endeavors.

As noted in the chapters on Cragfont and Rosemont, Jackson was a close friend of James Winchester and Jo Conn Guild, and he became acquainted with other early Sumner County luminaries—most notably those who were breeding and racing Thoroughbred horses. It was here in Sumner County that Jackson developed a near obsession with the burgeoning leisure sport of horse racing, a lifelong passion for Jackson.

Little is known of the businesses that were contained in the old building after Jackson went on to other pursuits. but we do know that during the Civil War, it was used as a surgery for soldiers from both North and South who were brought by train from battles in such places as Bowling Green and Perryville, Kentucky. In fact, during the worst of the war in Middle Tennessee, virtually every private home, public building and church in the area was housing recuperating wounded.

But the surgery was not a place where an injured soldier was going to quietly recover from dysentery or respiratory ailments with rest and hydrating fluids, nursed by nurturing women of the town. This was where those with limbs that needed to be amputated, serious head wounds, blown-out intestines and holes from the crude and deadly minie balls came to be attended to—and most likely, they would die here.

In the South, the general practitioners of the medical profession were ill-equipped to deal with battle wounds, and most had never even treated a gunshot wound, much less a shattered limb requiring amputation.

The sufferings of the sick and wounded in the hospitals strained the courage of the men and women of the South.

The first soldier buried in Gallatin City Cemetery's Confederate Cemetery was an "unknown" who arrived in Gallatin by train car and had been treated for a serious head wound at the surgery but died. The only clues as to who the young man had been or where he had called home were the buttons on his Confederate uniform: pewter pelicans, which signified a Louisiana regiment.

Roehrig recounts his first weeks at his new office, the remodeling and the discovery of blood stains on the floor of an interior room when new carpet was installed. "We couldn't keep the doors to that room shut," he remembered. "They would simply fly open, even if securely latched. This room contained our copy machine room and my law library, and upon discovering the old blood stains, we decided that this must be the room where the actual surgeries were performed. No doubt, in the heat of summer, the doctor would have wanted the doors open so air could circulate."

Roehrig is a sturdy, ruddy-faced man with sky-blue eyes, thick sandy hair and a full beard and mustache. In fact, he looks like he would be right at home in a Confederate uniform, on a horse, with a saber in his hand. His office is full of art depicting Civil War battles, and his friends and colleagues know that the way to put a smile on Roehrig's face is to bring him some relic from the war or an old magazine with an obscure firsthand account of a battle. "That's why I don't understand why these 'haints' like to bother me. If they are from the war days, they should know I am right there with them in spirit," Roehrig lamented.

He quickly found after moving into the building that it didn't matter how many times he turned the light in the stairwell off, "When I closed up for the night, by the time I got to the parking lot, it was back on."

"My radio would not stay tuned to my rock and roll station; it was constantly changing."

And then there were the clients—the "sensitive" ones who brought out activity of a paranormal nature. "We'd be sitting, discussing their case, and they would startle and say, 'There's somebody behind you, Mr. Roehrig.'" Several times, the "someone" was a little girl who has also been seen by paranormal investigators and, finally, by Roehrig himself.

Lori Snook, a paralegal assistant to attorney Bryan Roehrig, sits on the steps at Roehrig and Associates, the former law office of Andrew Jackson on the Gallatin Public Square and the site of a Civil War surgery. *Author's collection.*

Noises, bumps, taps on the shoulder when no one is there are all part of any working day at Roehrig's. The receptionist has seen a man in a black suit with a high, starched white collar sitting in the front lobby. When he is approached, he disappears into thin air.

And then there is the one incident that resulted in Bryan's decision to not stay at work past dark. "I had a client come in at 6:00 p.m. on a dark winter night when the sun sets at 4:45 p.m. in these parts," he explained. "We were in my office at the front of the building, and this guy was telling me that he had heard all the spooky stories about my building and he didn't believe 'in that silly stuff.'… About that time, we heard a big commotion in the back of the building. We ran back there, thinking someone had broken into the building, only to see aluminum cans from the recycling bin being hurled at the wall with tremendous force, making a huge racket, and not a person in sight," Roehrig chuckled. "My client headed for the front door, never to be seen again, and at that point, I decided never again to work after dark. I said to myself—and probably out loud to 'them'—'Hey, y'all can have it after dark, but leave me alone until then.'"

Roehrig's secretaries early on were eager to determine just who was haunting the office, so Roehrig made the same mistake Lowell Fayna did at Cragfont. He allowed Ouija board sessions. "Which, of course, was a mistake, because activity picked up, and soon, we were occasionally seeing a crying woman in a pale yellow, hoop-skirted dress float through the building, along with the little girl."

Since the building had been a surgical hospital during the Civil War, these apparitions did not, at first, make a lot of sense to Roehrig. "But the Ouija board session where a man identified himself as a Union teamster who didn't like anyone when he was living and 'sure didn't like anyone now,' helped me make the decision to not allow Ouija boards or any of that sort of thing from then on," said Roehrig.

"After that, occasionally, a client or a secretary would say a man's voice, 'rough and crude' had whispered in her ear, and it was ungentlemanly talk is all I am going to say about that," Roehrig snorted.

Sometimes, a client would report seeing a teenage boy, small and thin, in a Confederate uniform and cap who would grin and then disappear. Often, the boy was seen behind the office, just outside in the parking lot, and other times, he was seen in the hallway outside of Roehrig's office.

Roehrig instantly became intrigued, because this was a spirit with whom he could identify, given that he was a Civil War buff and member of the Sons of Confederate Veterans. He asked the client for as accurate a description as she could give, and she was able to describe the boy down to his hair color and complexion. Roehrig described his appearance to a historian friend who is familiar with uniforms and troop rosters, and the friend did research among the records of who had died in Gallatin at the surgery and had been buried in Confederate Circle.

Jesse B. Rowe, age seventeen, enlisted with Terry's Texas Rangers in Houston, Texas, in September 1861, and less than two months later, he was discharged in Bowling Green, Kentucky, due to chronic illness: consumption. He died in late November, around the time Paine took charge in Gallatin, at the surgery overlooking the gallows on the courthouse square. He was five feet, six inches tall, with light auburn hair, a fair complexion and blue eyes, which is exactly how he is described by those who have seen him—if only briefly.

The Pale Lady

The "Pale Lady," a woman in a faded yellow dress with even lighter hair, has been seen in various locations around Gallatin from city hall and the children's wing at the hospital to the Roehrig Law Office. She appears to be an entity without a permanent location or a particular time frame, although she does have a long dress, high-necked collar and sleeves common to the Civil War period.

Chris Alexander and his friend were riding their bikes on East Main Street one late Saturday night when they stopped at a grocery store for a soda. Gallatin is deserted after 11:00 p.m. most nights, so the presence of an older woman in a long dress, high lace collar and long, tousled, whitish hair in the middle of the street startled the boys. In a small, close-knit community, the street characters are well known by sight, if not by name. This woman was not someone the boys knew or had seen before.

She was a flesh-and-blood apparition; no part of her was transparent, and she easily locked eyes with the boys. "Please help me; I am looking for my daughter, and I need to give her this," said the woman, holding out her hand, which contained a small bottle. "Can you help me?" she repeated. The boys looked at each other and then the woman and shook their heads. "We haven't seen your daughter," they replied.

The boys got back on their bikes and continued home, but Alexander said, "Was she a ghost?" They both laughed because, although they couldn't quite wrap their heads around what had just happened, at the time, they did not consider the supernatural. Still, Alexander said, "Let's see where she went."

The two boys canvassed the area on their bikes; if the woman was on foot, she would be no match in speed for fifteen-year-olds on bikes. But she was nowhere to be found. The boys were really puzzled, and they were beginning to lean more toward the paranormal as an explanation.

Chris Alexander stands where he and his friend saw the Pale Lady when they were teenagers, riding bikes on East Main Street in Gallatin. *Author's collection.*

Being teenagers, an age when every day is a new day and strange things you see during the night fade away with the morning, the incident was forgotten, and it was ten years before Alexander thought about the unusual happenings of that night again.

He was attending the Gallatin Ghost Walk History and Mystery Tour, and the tour presenter was talking about the "mysterious lady in pale yellow with whitish hair" that is seen all over central Gallatin, asking for her daughter. "That's when it hit me," Alexander said. "That's what we saw that night."

Who could this woman be? What remnant of the past does she represent?

Perhaps the key to the mystery lies in the happenings of late August 1862.

A brief recap of the Civil War as it pertains to the events in Sumner County begins with the fall of Fort Donelson in West Tennessee in February 1862, which left Middle Tennessee unprotected and vulnerable to Union forces.

Eager for a stronghold and control of the interstate railroad that ran right through Sumner County, Union troops flooded the area and quickly realized the strategic location of the town.

Equally eager to attack the federal supply lines were guerrilla raiders and the troops under the command of Confederate general John Hunt Morgan, whose daring exploits in and around Sumner County made him a folk hero to a beleaguered populace.

In March 1862, the Union pulled troops from Gallatin to fight in the Battle of Shiloh in extreme southern Tennessee; it was a brief respite for weary Sumner Countians, but the peace would not last for long, and troops returned in early summer.

In early August Morgan captured Gallatin for the Confederacy, and the Union departed in humiliation but vowing vengeance on a Rebel citizenry. Subsequently, Morgan blew up Big South Tunnel on the L&N Railroad line and delayed Union supplies to the south for ninety days.

Shortly thereafter, Union troops arrived in Gallatin and "rampaged through town in retribution," according to Mary Robertson Schell, who, like Alice Williamson, kept a brief diary of events during these tumultuous times. Schell was the wife of a jeweler in Gallatin, and the family lived at the juncture of Hartsville Pike and the Old Scottsville Pike, near where the Sav-a-Lot Grocery Store is located today. Their location gave them front-row seats to the comings and goings of troops north and south into and out of the city and to the Battle of Gallatin, which occurred on August 21, 1862. "At an early hour in the morning [of August 13] the [federal] artillery came rushing through the streets...yelling and cursing in the most violent manner; they dashed past our residence....They rushed into houses, insulting the inmates, ordering the servants to get provisions for them...stealing everything they could carry off; they then broke open the stores and destroyed what they could not carry," including drugstore items, sorely needed by a population under embargo with goods scarce and at black market prices if they could be had at all. On August 19, a group of Union scouts, angered at the damage along the railroad from South Tunnel to Gallatin, "came into town and left with 130 male citizens, most of the men of the town, as prisoners."

At this point in the war, any able-bodied Sumner County man between the ages of sixteen and fifty was in the Confederate ranks, and only the very old, the very young or infirm were left in town. Nevertheless, the Union troops marched the men toward Nashville, taking any money or watches they had on their persons, forcing them to walk on the uneven and precarious railroad tracks, poking them in the back with bayonets when they did not move quickly enough and denying them water in the hot summer sun.

Schell's own husband was among those forced to march. She gave an account of this seizing of citizens: "[O]ne of the soldiers came running up to our door, inquiring if any men were in this house; on being assured there was not, he left to run to other houses in quest of men and boys; after all the male citizens had been collected, they were…taken to Nashville.…A desperate scene of outrage [among the women ensued]."

Morgan had a reputation for his intolerance of cruelty to civilians, and when word of this atrocity reached him, he rescued most of the prisoners, took two hundred Union troops captive and returned triumphant to Gallatin with most of the formerly captive male citizenry in tow. Schell's husband was not among them, but he and the others who did not return with Morgan did reach Gallatin in the days that followed.

These tumultuous events culminated in the Battle of Gallatin on August 21, a fight that only lasted for about an hour and occurred around Dr. Blackmore's homestead, Blythewood, which still stands on Hartsville Pike.

The wounded, both Union and Confederate, were treated in homes nearby and at Transmontania Male Academy behind the Carriage House Factory on what is today East Main Street, directly across the street from the grocery store where Chris Alexander and his friend saw the Pale Lady.

Mary Schell wrote, "Saturday 23rd, I have been to the male academy which the federals have taken for a hospital and is now the general reception for the wounded; several deaths have already occurred, the wounds being fatal. The ladies of both town and country are very assiduous and faithful in their administrations. I have been administering to their wants." Mrs. Schell's daughter was at the academy, assisting the wounded.

Is it possible that what Alexander and his friend saw that night was a snapshot of that distant time, when women would have been carrying home-made tinctures and decoctions to the hospital for use by the wounded? Was the woman needing to get the vial in her hand to her daughter at the academy or a private home where the wounded were being attended?

The Union naval blockade prevented ships carrying medical supplies from reaching southern states, so they turned to the old tried and true herbal remedies of their forebears. "Lacking the industry available in the North for synthesizing compounds, the South relied much more heavily on homegrown ingredients and remedies, and attention was dedicated to finding the equivalent natural alternatives to ingredients that were not available in the South.…Many soldiers and surgeons would search the

A lithograph of a typical scene in the North and South during the Civil War, as women opened their homes to the sick and wounded. *Courtesy of* Harper's Weekly.

fields and forests for remedies that they remembered their mothers and grandmothers using," said Janet M. Brown in her book *Herbal Use in the American Civil War*.

Did the Pale Lady search her own garden for medicinal herbs, make a "potion" and attempt delivery to where it was needed to aid the wounded?

She is seen at Sumner Regional Hospital at times and in downtown Gallatin, usually in front of the former surgery on the east side of the square, so it seems she is indeed on a medical mission of mercy.

Random paranormal phenomena occur all over the Gallatin Public Square, even if some occupants are reluctant to talk about it. In the old bank building at the corner of West Main Street and the public square, paranormal activity has occurred for years. The building, built post–Civil War, had been a bank for one hundred years before it became offices for lawyers and other professionals. Lowell Fayna remembers when the building was vacant, around 1999. "It was Christmastime, and I had a key and permission to store food and toys in there for a charity giveaway," he reported. "I'd go in, and my food and toys had been moved around, and things had other items piled on top of them. Sometimes, the boxes would have been hidden," he went on to say. In the 1930s, a man hanged himself on the second story. Employees who worked in the building in the 1980s were hesitant to go into the basement due to paranormal activity there. In 2019, the Nightstalkers, paranormal investigators, took a stab at determining the cause of the phenomena and failed to reach any definite conclusions, although their equipment was disturbed during the investigation after picking up voices and noises.

Just one block north of the square is Franklin Street. For over one hundred years, the Boyers House dominated the block with its two-story white pillars and white clapboard façade. It was the home and dance studio of "Miss" Betsy Boyers from about 1920 to 1970, when the house was demolished. Many Sumner County residents who learned ballet, tap or ballroom dance received instruction from the colorful and vivacious Miss Betsy, who was an accomplished ballerina and had trained in New York City before returning home to Gallatin, where her family's roots run deep.

Miss Betsy stood only about five feet tall and had a severe, Cleopatra-style haircut with ebony bangs and bright, intelligent eyes. While Miss Betsy was known for being plain-spoken and blunt when the occasion called for it, her students adored her, and her recitals and studio open houses were community events.

But students and even grown-ups avoided her home after dark when possible, due to the notorious reputation of it being haunted, both by unseen poltergeist-type manifestations and, occasionally, a boisterous but harmless Confederate ghost. "People will say I am crazy, and they can believe what they wish," Miss Betsy told a newspaper reporter from the *Nashville Tennessean* in an interview in 1970. The article reported that Miss Betsy "has lived in the house since a child and has heard many noises but has never seen any ghosts. However, other friends and relatives have reported seeing them."

Miss Betsy said many other people thought they saw someone walk by the windows, but when they investigated, there was no one there. "One afternoon, Sam Lackey and his brother Dr. Lackey were visiting the house, and a transom over the door began to make a very loud noise and flapped as if someone was trying to knock it down. Well, Dr. Lackey and his brother quickly excused themselves to go home," laughed Miss Betsy.

Miss Betsy reported that when she first began converting parts of the house into a dance studio, Dr. Lackey had taken her into Nashville one afternoon to pick up some supplies. As they drove up in front of the house that night, they heard a noise that sounded like a group of men hammering on the back of the house, but nothing could be found after a thorough search. The noises began again as they went to the front of the house, and they went back and forth from the front of the house to the back but could never find the noise.

Miss Betsy heard footsteps on her stairs and her screen doors bang in the middle of the night, "as if people were running in and out." She would get up to check the doors, and they would all be latched. "Uncle Charlie" is the name she gave to a ghost visitors saw dressed in a Confederate uniform and carrying a sword who appeared quite frequently, walking to a bedroom window and pulling open the curtain. "And if anyone is sleeping there, he stomps around and awakens them, then stares at the person who, by that time, is awake and scared quite out of their wits," said Miss Betsy.

Melvin Brazzell knew Miss Betsy back in the day and remembers a friend of his who spent the night at the Boyers home and woke up in the night to see two women in long, hoop skirt dresses sitting at a table by lamplight, sewing and rolling bandages, something that certainly would have been done in the days of the occupation of Gallatin during the Civil War. "One of the women looked up from her task and said, 'What are you doing awake?' before disappearing into thin air," Brazzell chuckled.

Roberta Hancock remembers being a young girl who attended Miss Betsy's dance school. "It was not at all unusual for students to see something or someone spectral flit by out of the corner of our eyes during dance class," she said. "The house was always 'active' and seemed to be especially noticeable when Miss Betsy had her twice-yearly ballroom dancing classes in the main parlor of the home," Hancock recalled.

Gallatin resident and artist/illustrator Jeff Preston is blond, athletic and affable with a fondness for sci-fi, the macabre and practical jokes. His creative endeavors extend beyond his professional art career, as he has conducted no less than three haunted house venues in years past—two on the square in Gallatin and one in Nashville. He also hosted a popular but short-lived dinner theater on Gallatin's public square.

When Preston was creating each of the haunted house venues on the square, he said, "Naturally, our imaginations worked overtime." He added, "Anytime we were there at night, it was spooky. It wasn't hard to imagine all sorts of things, what with old mannequins from the building's former life as

Jeff Preston operated "Terror on the Square," a haunted attraction loosely based on the legend of Lackey's Caves and the harsh reality of the Reign of Terror of the Union occupation, led by General Eleazar Paine, during the Civil War. *Author's collection.*

a menswear store silhouetted against the windows and the odd creak of a century-old structure with several staircases and original wood floors."

"I think the story we chose for the second haunted house season brought on some of what happened that was definitely of an unexplained nature," said Preston. "I'm always a skeptic until I see something I can't explain." Preston used the General Eleazer Paine atrocities and the local legend of Lackey's Caves to craft a terrifying story of death and gore in a subterranean world. "We started hearing footsteps for real that year. It was not anyone's imagination," said Preston. "At one point, a psychic ghosthunter called us and wanted to come check out the property." He added, "She stood right where we had heard footsteps and grabbed her head and shoulders, as if in pain; later, we did some research and found that the Confederate veteran who had been the owner of the building long ago had a missing arm and other injuries from wounds he suffered in the war."

Another incident was worthy of a Jeff Preston master prank, but he said it "was absolutely real, and I had nothing to do with it," he laughed. "We had brought a landline telephone to the building to be connected later. It wasn't even plugged in....One evening, it rang," said Preston, "which pretty much freaked everyone out, including me."

Once the venue was open to the public, the strange occurrences did not stop. "One night, a visitor to the haunted house said, 'Hey, who was that guy in the Confederate uniform?' He didn't seem to have a part," Preston remembered. "Well, we didn't have anyone in the scenario at the haunted house wearing a Confederate uniform," Preston said. "They were seeing something that wasn't one of our actors or guests, but that's OK; we were there to entertain, and the less special effects we have to pay for, the better!" said Preston with his characteristic wit.

The courthouse itself is home to a ghost known as Stinky. According to Adam Blai, a consultant in demonology and exorcism for the Catholic Diocese of Pittsburgh, signs of demonic infestation include "bad odors… strong and very revolting. The odor does not dissipate and does not linger where the demon was; it moves with it."

Rebecca Groves remembers her parents talking about a foul stench that accompanied paranormal activity at the Sumner County Courthouse, located on the public square in Gallatin. Both of her parents and other

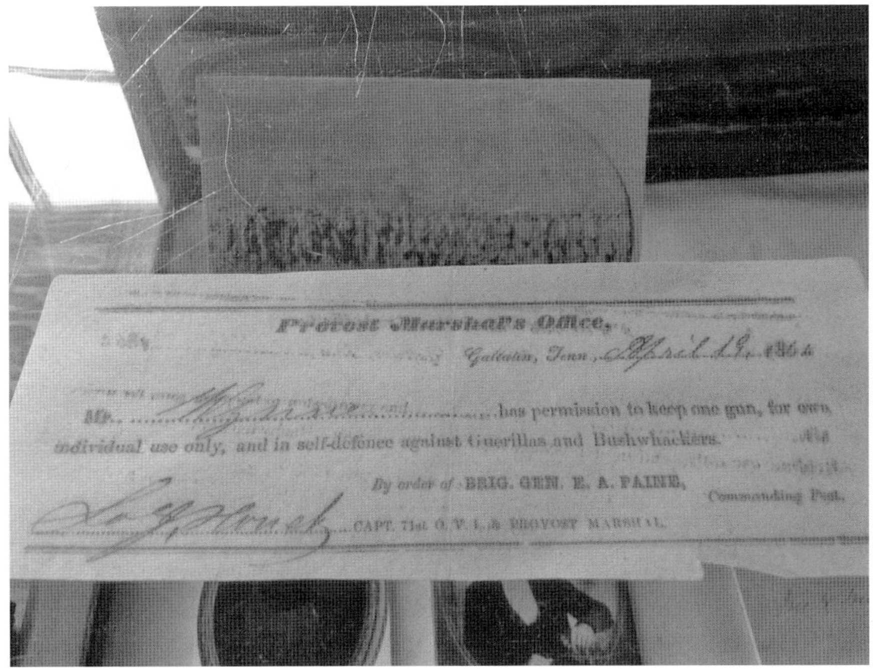

A photograph of the pass granted to Alfred Wynne, a veteran of the Revolutionary War and an early Sumner County settler, by the Union provost marshal of the occupying forces, granting him the right to own one gun for the purpose of defending his property. *Author's photogrpah, Wynnewood collection.*

family members worked as janitorial staff, cleaning the post–Depression era structure, which stands where two previous courthouse buildings have stood, including the infamous courthouse that served as General Paine's headquarters for occupied Gallatin during the Civil War. "They would come home with just so many stories," remembered Rebecca. "They would walk into an office inside the courthouse to clean it and books would be open, but upon leaving the room, those books would be closed....There were sounds of people running up and down the stairs, but the courthouse was locked, and the janitors were the only ones in the place," said Rebecca. "Elevators would run, stop on different floors, open, and there would be no one inside."

But the most notable and baffling occurrence was the presence of an odor so foul and strong that the fire department had to be called, and Rebecca's mother, an asthmatic, became ill and had to leave the building, despite opening all the windows on the floor where they were working.

Two blocks west of the Public Square, the Gallatin Police Department occupies a 1970s structure across from the fire station. Samantha Davis worked as a dispatcher for the department. "I used to take my breaks up in the patrol room, which was always empty about midnight," she remembered. "That is where the office cat, Taser, stayed, and I liked to pet him and just get away from the busy dispatch center," Davis went on to say. "One night, when I rounded the corner by the short staircase, I saw the shape of a person," Davis recalled. "If you have ever seen a spirit, you know it happens so fast, like a snapshot of something or someone, but you have just enough time to get a general idea of who they are and what they look like," she said.

"This was a police officer, and he seemed baffled at the presence of the doors at the top of the stairs," Davis explained. "As if he were saying, 'What are these doing here?'...Well, those doors weren't always there. They were added at some point," Davis noted. "Whoever he was, he didn't know about those doors."

"The area became extremely cold when the apparition appeared," Davis said. "But it was gone as quickly as it had come....Of course, I went back to my workstation, and I told everyone there. The officers teased me and generally said I was 'seeing things,' but one of them did believe me....He took it seriously enough to go with me to the wall of memorial photos of officers who died in the line of duty, and when I saw one photo in particular,

The Gallatin Public Square, like most courthouse squares in America, has always been a place of unity in trying times. Pictured here is a gathering that took place just after September 11, 2001. Citizens came to sign a large banner of support and encouragement for the first responders of the New York City Police and Fire Departments. *Author's collection.*

The third courthouse to be located on the Gallatin Public Square was built in the 1930s as part of a Works Progress Administration program. The construction of a fourth courthouse is underway, as evidenced by the crane in the background, but for the first time in over two hundred years, this courthouse will not be on the square. *Author's collection.*

I just got cold chills and cried," said Davis. "I had a true sense of recognition when I saw this one particular officer's photograph….I think maybe the officer who believed me about seeing a spirit had maybe seen it, too, but it would not have gone over well for him to be telling that to the rest of the brotherhood….I know what I saw," Davis asserted.

Next door to the police station is Chubb's Sports Bar and Grill, located in the building that was once the firehouse, in the days when horses pulled water wagons to fires. When they were not being used to fight blazes, the horse-drawn wagons served as trash collection vehicles. In the past forty-plus years, the two-story brick building with central staircase has been home to several popular and diverse restaurants, and there have always been stories of equipment and cutlery moving about by themselves, noises on the stairs and a shadowy figure or two.

Jenny Campos had just recently moved to Gallatin from California when she found employment at Chubb's as part of their team of enthusiastic, young and attractive waitstaff. After only a few weeks on the job, with the subject of Chubb's "activity" never coming up, Jenny was unprepared for what occurred one afternoon as she was clearing dishes from the tables in the outdoor patio area. Her hands were full of dishes and glassware on a tray, and she was prepared to reenter the restaurant when she hesitated a moment to adjust her load so that she could open the glass-paneled door. Before she had a chance to grasp the doorhandle, an "arm" without a body attached to it reached across Jenny and opened the door. "I just couldn't really process what I was seeing," said Jenny. And like most paranormal encounters, it happened very quickly.

"I stopped and asked the first waiter I saw, 'Hey, did you just come through here? Did you see a man open the door?'" she recounted. "I guess he thought that was a strange question for a busy day in a busy restaurant," laughed Jenny. The waiter said he had not seen anyone near the door and that, to his knowledge, he had been the only one who had walked through there—and he had not opened the door for her.

Just across the alley from Chubb's and fronting North Water Street are two businesses separated by a long, two-story, open foyer that runs from Water Street to a parking lot in the back. This was the location of the city's livery stables during much of the nineteenth century. Since it was recently renovated into a central, open, arcade-style space, with offices on either side of the expansive center space, it is not hard to visualize that horses could be stabled below, with hay stored above to be thrown down to the stock as needed.

After the stable was closed, a live-in hotel upstairs was divided into many small rooms for rent, leading to the pervasive local legend that the structure was a brothel, although no historic evidence of that exists. It is known,

Chubb's Sports Bar is located where the old firehouse used to be. During the late 1800s, the entire west side of the square burned three times. *Author's collection.*

however, that bootlegging occurred in the alley behind the structure on Enlow Street in the 1950s.

In January 2020, Debby Locke and other artists in the area opened an artists' cooperative, the Artisan Hatchery, in one of the spaces fronting Water Street. Locke said the space was relatively free of any incidents that could be seen as paranormal until October that year. "As I was leaving one evening, at dark, I had gone all the way to the back of the foyer and was about to lock the back door and get into my car when I saw a man, woman and child standing inside the front door of the building," she recalled. "I came back in the building and walked down the long hall to get a better look," Locke remembered. "And that's when I saw the full-bodied apparitions of the man, woman and child, although the man was much more distinct, and it was he who actually locked eyes with me," she said. Locke described the woman and child as "not as clearly defined" as the man, who had "tailored clothes; a vest, perhaps striped; and something red. They all remained there until people passed by on the sidewalk just outside the door, and they disappeared, only to reappear once the passersby were gone," she noted.

"I went back to my car, because at that point, I realized I wasn't seeing 'real' people," Locke said. "I got in my Jeep and shined the headlights through the glass door, illuminating the foyer all the way to the front....The three 'people' were still there....I just left," Locke said.

Not long after that, what Locke refers to as the "Pennywise incident" occurred. "It was October, and I had done a painting of just the eyes of Pennywise, the demonic clown from Stephen King's *It*, as well as some paintings of evil-eyed jack-o'-lanterns," said Locke. "They were hanging on the north wall of the gallery....My friend was here in the back of the shop after closing time, and he heard something up front. Upon investigating, he observed the Pennywise painting face-up on the floor, a good five feet from the wall where it had been hung," said Locke. "He thought it was odd, but he re-hung it. But a few days later, it was back off the wall, sitting upright against the wall, below where it had been hanging," remembered Locke.

"What was so startling is that the hanging cord had been cut—not frayed but cut," Locke remarked, adding that this was all so disturbing that "*Pennywise* is now in my storeroom. I don't want that painting here or in my home." Since it is a quality work of art, some surrounding stores have expressed interest in buying *Pennywise*. "That painting just does not belong on this square," said Locke.

Debby Locke painted "Pennywise" the sadistic clown from Stephen King's book and movie *It*. Pennywise refused to stay hung on the wall. *Author's collection.*

Across the foyer from the artists' cooperative is the former home of Pristine Pup, a dog grooming establishment. Katrina Lamb made renovations to the space prior to moving in, including constructing a dividing wall, a tub with special plumbing suitable for dog bathing and other improvements. Throughout the weeks prior to the establishment's opening, "We had a feeling that someone was always watching us," said Lamb. "The kind of feeling where you just want to turn around to see who is there but no one ever is," she went on to say.

Even after opening the shop, the presence never receded. "At least once a week when my daughter and I were there, we would each hear the other calling our names—only neither of us had called out to the other," Lamb said. "One of the freakiest things that happened was early one morning when I came in alone to open up. We have a black rubberized floor in the bathing area. There were fresh, wet, adult-sized footprints all over the mat," she added. "When I told my daughter, she said, 'Mom, I told you this place was haunted!'"

Even the dogs that wait in dog crates to be groomed or picked up by their owners are not immune to seeing things, according to Lamb. "One day, all the dogs went crazy at once; in every single kennel, the dogs were turning their heads in unison, as if watching something go back and forth, back and forth on the wall....Our grooming scissors often went missing and then turned up in weird places," Lamb noted. "We had security cameras and would find the scissors in places where it should be visible on the security camera that they have been picked up and moved, but the cameras never pick it up."

"One day, my grandson, age three, came in the back door of the building [the same back door that leads to the long foyer where Debby Locke saw the apparitions] and looked up at the second-story balcony and said, 'Can I go play with those kids?'" Lamb, seeing no children and then aware of the extent of the paranormal activity, said her response was, "'Never. No.'...He was confused, and ever after that, when we came in that back door, he would look up and laugh and act like he saw someone up there."

Lamb isn't frightened by the activity. "The footprints were the most disturbing. The rest just seems like something a child—perhaps a ghost child—would do just to play tricks," she believes.

Mysterious Fires

In late April 1880, the entire west side of the Gallatin Public Square burned at 3:00 a.m., believed to be the "work of tramps who were seen loitering around town yesterday," according to the *Cincinnati Daily Star*. Insurance covered the $20,000 loss.

On July 12, 1899, and again, less than a week later, on July 16, fires destroyed first the west side and then the entire south side of the square.

From the *Nashville Tennessean* on July 13, 1899:

> *The most destructive fire that has visited this place in many years occurred this morning. At 2:30 a.m., the fire bell tapped, and the citizens of the town rushed to the public square to find that the Nicholson Drug Store in the west side block was on fire. The fire company responded to a man, and every effort possible was made to stop the flames, but all efforts were futile until the flames had destroyed six business houses and had consumed the row of business houses from Franklin Street in the public square, which was the best business portion of the town.*
>
> *The origin of the fire is a mystery.*

Although the Nashville Fire Department was summoned to aid the town of Gallatin, which had no waterworks at the time, Gallatin was able to extinguish the fire. When the engines from Nashville arrived, there was no need for them to unload their equipment. A brisk wind in the opposite direction saved the square and businesses on Water Street from complete destruction.

Four days later, the south side of the square was also wiped out by a fire that originated in a shed. The post office was burned, but the mail was saved. The Tompkins Opera House was a total loss.

The Nicholson Drug Company, twice burned, is quite likely the same location of the later drugstore, Swaney-Swift, which, today, is a popular restaurant.

Thankfully, no lives were lost in any of the fires on the square, so for answers to the pervasive mystery of ghostly children at the Hatchery as well as at Swaney-Swift, we will have to turn to the several epidemics, each of which killed approximately 15 percent of the population of Sumner County, many of them children.

Travis and Kimberly Roberts are owners of Swaney-Swift, a restaurant in the location of the old Swaney-Swift drugstore, located in what is most

Swaney-Swift owners Travis and Kimberly Roberts say there are things they cannot explain that occur daily in the historic Swaney-Swift Drugstore, now restaurant. They have named the resident spirit Sarah and believe her to be a mischievous child ghost. *Author's collection.*

likely the same building that was the Nicholson Drugstore. Travis says his building was used as a doctor's office and infirmary for many of the cholera and smallpox epidemics that decimated Sumner County in the last half of the nineteenth century and into the twentieth century. "Specifically, we feel that the mischievous spirit is a little girl, and we have named her Sarah," he smiled.

"Sarah" is enamored of a small doll, a "pew-doll" made out of a lace handkerchief, a traditional plaything that was acceptable to be taken to church, because playing with such a doll would not make any noise like porcelain or cast plaster would. "We have no idea when that doll came here to the restaurant or where it came from," said Kimberly, "only that we can find it in one location downstairs one day, lock up for the night and come in the next day and it has moved upstairs to the office."

Travis noted, "There are things I can't explain away, and I'm the biggest skeptic there is....Lights will flicker but maybe only two at a time; the rest will be fine. The ice bucket will fly off the shelf. The tea machine's top will fly off and land across the room," he added.

On the stairs leading to the upstairs office, "there are footsteps but no one there," said Kimberly. "The pendant light will swing. Sometimes, on

Swaney-Swift has been a familiar sight on the west side of the Gallatin Public Square since the mid-twentieth century. In years past, it had a soda fountain and gift shop and filled prescriptions. Today, it is a popular restaurant, still offering hamburgers and milkshakes. *Author's collection.*

my desktop security camera monitor, a hazy, thin wisp will cross one of the frames on the monitor—just one—and the location of the mist varies."

Travis said, "Thuds and bumps that are investigated find no one there and nothing amiss, nothing having fallen." He added, "We will have locked up for the night, and our alarm will go off, summoning the police, who then find nothing amiss."

"We feel Sarah is a gentle spirit," said Kimberly. But like many people living or working on the west side of the square, the Robertses wonder about the origin of so many apparitions and manifestations of children.

A Nurturing Spirit

The charming Italianate cottage at the south end of College Street, just two blocks off the square, is the former parsonage for Cumberland Presbyterian Church, which was active until the late 1800s in Gallatin. Its distinctive twin doors behind a broad porch lead some to believe it was built as a duplex, but that is not the case. The entries were designed that way so the pastor of the church could have one entrance into his study for parishioners' use, and the other door was solely for his family to use to access their residence.

The resident spirit is gentle. She is nurturing, if not a bit headstrong about where occupants place furniture and objects, and she apparently only appears to children, although adults hear and feel her presence through the way objects move and occasionally soar through the air, as if thrown.

The little house has been a private residence for most of its 120 years—that is, until a series of cafés and restaurants began to open there in 2008.

Mark and Carol Johnson spent many hours at the site, assisting their daughter Meredith with her café from 2011 to 2012. "There is a definite feminine presence in the house," said Carol. "Most notably, the presence of flowers seemed to bring out the paranormal activity," she went on to say. "We put fresh flowers in little vases centered on the tables every morning. We had a chalkboard on the porch where we would write the specials of the day, and when we would come back in from writing on the chalk board, the flower vases would have all been moved to the corners of the tables in the two dining rooms," Carol added. "There were also scratching sounds that would come from the bathroom and on the floors and the spiral staircase before we had even opened to the public," remembered Carol.

The "little house on College Street" is an Italianate cottage with a nurturing spirit, its resident ghost. Kelley Cassetty and Don Ostrander are the owners/ proprietors of Best Eats Café and Catering. *Author's collection.*

The steep, winding, metal spiral staircase goes from the first floor to the basement and was unused by the public, largely because it was hard to navigate. It was roped off so that it would not be explored. The Johnsons' two-year-old granddaughter was often in the restaurant after closing time, and as toddlers are apt to do, she could be clinging to Carol's leg one minute and off and running the next. "The staircase was something we had to watch if children were around, because a very small child would not have been able to manage its twists and turns, and the open space between steps would create a real hazard. So, the day my granddaughter was suddenly not in sight, we immediately ran to the staircase," Carol said. "Which is why we were so astonished to find my granddaughter perfectly safe and sound, unhurt and not crying or upset, at the bottom of that spiral staircase," Carol said, still in disbelief. "How did she get there that fast and totally uninjured?" wondered Carol.

"When I picked her up, she turned to the dark, empty basement room and stared at one corner, waving and saying, 'Bye, lady,'" said Carol. "She saw someone the rest of us didn't see, and it was a nonthreatening, even friendly, 'someone.'" Did the nurturing and "feminine" spirit rescue the child from a fall on the stairs? Did she pick her up and place her at the foot of the precarious steps?

After almost a year in the little house, word about the spirit or spirits in the house had gotten around among the Johnsons' friends, and one night at a private dinner in the café, "our friends were laughing about all the phenomena, making light of it," said Carol. "Suddenly, the heavy lid on a large stock pot, which was cooking soup on the stove, flew across the room like a frisbee," asserted Carol.

The café was open for just over two years, and after its closing, a succession of businesses and residents have followed—with some saying there is a "presence," if not an actual spirit, and others declining to comment.

Nevertheless, the "lady" may just be waiting for the right occupants to reassert herself.

Those who remember visiting the house as children, when the occupant babysat children in the home, recall some children talking about "that other lady," as distinguished from their babysitter, from time to time, according to Carol.

Subsequent residents remember a "presence" that was not at all threatening but would, however, move objects. And once, in the dead of winter, a resident who was home alone in her basement bedroom awoke, cold and unable to find her comforter. It had been folded in a neat square at the bottom of her bed.

~

From all over Sumner County come the tales of occurrences that cannot be explained by rational, logical means, and many of these tales are centered on soldiers who seem to be lost or detached from their regiments.

Angie McCracken grew up on an old wagon road in Sugar Grove. "Legend is that soldiers camped in what is now our front yard," Angie said. "One Easter, the family had all gathered for the holiday, and my mom and I took a break to walk our dogs just at sunset....We had gone a little way down the road when, suddenly, the hair on the dogs' backs stood straight up. In front of us was a soldier wearing all blue; he was shaggy-haired and dirty and limped a little," reported Angie. "We were startled; we didn't know what to think and ran back and got the family to help us search for the man. We never found any trace of him."

James Rice lives in Castalian Springs on Greenfield Lane in a home that was built in the 1980s. One afternoon, his daughter came home from the grocery store and, to her surprise, saw a Union soldier on the front porch. He disappeared as she approached.

Bloodstains on the floors of antebellum structures allude to the fact that most homes of that era in Sumner County served, at least for some time, as hospitals for injured soldiers.

On Greenfield Lane in Castalian Springs, Kristie Owens grew up in a house where "we saw and heard all kinds of things on that property."

> *At night, you could hear metal rattling and sometimes the sound of a tractor....There were bloodstains on the floor that would appear then disappear...Once, my dad had an encounter at the old well. As he was bending down to pick something up, he felt a presence right behind him, breathing on him....Once, in the barn, we came upon a rope hanging from the ceiling. It wasn't limp—it had obvious tension on it....Cattle wouldn't go in that barn.*

Postscript to War

John Muir, the great American wanderer, traveled across the northern Cumberland Plateau. Muir, whose countless quotes include, "The mountains are calling, and I must go," was a Scottish-born naturalist who migrated to the United States in 1849 and became a fierce advocate for the American wilderness. He's commonly referred to as the father of the U.S. National Parks Service, and he explored much of the country on foot.

In 1867, Muir set out from Louisville, Kentucky, headed for Cedar Key, Florida. His one-thousand-mile walk to the Gulf of Mexico was the first of his cross-country journeys of consequence, and it was his longest hike. It was on this walk that he crossed the Cumberland Plateau, describing the plants and people he met at length in his journal. The Cumberland Mountains, in fact, were the first mountains he had seen in his life—though he would go on to become perhaps best known for his exploration of the Rocky Mountains and many other mountain chains.

Muir's description of the Cumberland Plateau tells of isolated and desolate communities that had been ravaged by the Civil War, which had ended just a couple of years before his trek through the region. A 2019 article in the *Oneida, Tennessee Independent-Herald* said:

When Muir reached Jamestown, [Tennessee] *he called it a "poor, rickety, thrice-dead village…an incredibly dreary place." Nearby, he stopped at a log home to inquire about food and a place to sleep. He was turned away because he didn't have the correct change to pay for his accommodations—but not without a glass of milk. The woman at the home told him there was one home beyond hers, about two miles away, "but beyond that, there are no houses that I know of except empty ones whose owners have been killed or driven away during the war."…Muir found lodging at the next house.*

Before Muir left the home, the [man] *warned him against traveling deeper into the remote land, saying that small bands of guerrillas were hiding along the route, even though the war had ended.*

Muir didn't heed the man's advice, and when he continued his journey the next morning, September 11, 1867, he described the Cumberland Plateau landscape like this: "Long stretch of level sandstone plateau, lightly furrowed and dimpled with shallow groove-like valleys and hills. The trees are mostly oaks, planted far apart, like those in the Wisconsin woods. A good many pine trees here and there, forty to eighty feet high, and most of the ground is covered with showy flowers. Milkworts, goldenrods and asters were especially abundant. I came to a cool, clear brook every half mile or so, the banks planted with royal fern, cinnamon fern and handsome sedges. The few larger streams were fringed with laurels and azaleas. Large areas beneath the trees are covered with formidable green briers and brambles, armed with hooked claws, and almost impenetrable."

"Houses," Muir wrote, "are far apart and uninhabited, orchards and fences in ruins—sad marks of war."

4

CRYBABY BRIDGE AND GUERRILLA GHOSTS

Northern Sumner County is dotted with rolling hills, plenty of fertile land and small towns, each with populations under five thousand. Many have populations of five hundred or less. These are largely farming communities with residents whose families have been in the area for multiple generations. If residents don't farm, they are dependent on construction and trade jobs—or drive forty miles to either Nashville to the south or Bowling Green, Kentucky, to the north. Some work at the factories and industrial hubs in Portland or the county seat of Gallatin.

In these relatively isolated, tight-knit towns, there's not that much for the younger crowd to do on a Friday or Saturday night when it's not football season. Most do what kids with cars have done for decades in these largely rural communities—they hang out with friends, play cards or video games and ride around the winding country roads, waiting for some sort of excitement to present itself.

Marcus Keen, Joshua Johns and Jacob Burton were doing the latter one spring evening when they decided to check out a legend they had been hearing about for years. "It's come to be known as the Crybaby Bridge haunting," said Jacob, "and basically, it says if you go to a certain bridge at midnight, you will hear a baby cry and see the ghost of a woman jump from the bridge."

If one does an internet search for the term *crybaby bridge*, it will reveal no less than twenty such haunted places across the United States—so many that some call Crybaby Bridge an urban legend and myth that is propagated by overly imaginative teenagers with time on their hands.

It would follow that Marcus and his friends probably had a few beers, had heard the legend somewhere in the common ether of the teenage rumor mill, either online or in their own orbits, and, on a pitch-dark midnight in an isolated rural locale, acquire their own tale of hearing a crying baby on a spooky bridge. It doesn't help debunk the theory of "overactive imaginations" at work that the crying is rumored to begin precisely at midnight.

Jacob had been to the bridge "a couple of times" prior to enlisting his friends to go along. "I had always heard the story of the baby crying at the bridge; in fact, my dad told me he and his friends had always heard of it, too," he added. "Basically, the legend is that a woman and her baby drowned there in the mid-1900s. A variation on the story is that a woman in a car had a wreck, got out of the car and, somehow, the baby got in the water and she couldn't find him. He was found frozen to death on the banks of the creek several days later," said Jacob.

Another version says the woman threw the baby off the bridge, then leapt to her own death, but the distance from the bridge to the water is a mere twelve feet, so this seems an unlikely way to end one's life.

Marcus Keen said he and friend Josh "didn't believe Jacob about the hauntings at the bridge. I told him I'd have to see it to believe it."

What the three experienced the night they went to the bridge was "wild," according to Marcus. Josh added, "It gave me goosebumps. Still does. And I will not go back. Not ever."

Indeed, at precisely midnight, a baby cried—faintly, at first, and then a little louder.

"Then we heard footsteps on the bridge," said Marcus. Josh and Jacob said they heard the footsteps, too. Under the bridge is a "noisy brook," said Josh. It was in this flowing creek that all three men heard splashing, "as if people were running through the creek, turning over rocks or somehow making a lot of noise going through the shallow creek," he added. "It was just very out of the ordinary and not at all what we were expecting."

And then, sometime around 1:00 a.m., all three watched as a "black, smoky figure, female in form, about five feet, eight inches tall or taller, with long, wild hair jumped—then appeared to float—off the bridge," said Josh. He added, "This was my first real encounter with the paranormal....This was way out of my comfort zone."

Crybaby Bridge is located at the site of the headquarters of one of the Civil War's most notorious Confederate guerrilla fighters, Ellis Harper, and was the scene of a deadly skirmish between an Ohio regiment and Harper's men in June 1863. During the Civil War, guerrilla forces arose on both

Ellis Harper, an infamous Confederate guerrilla fighter and Partisan Ranger, made his headquarters just outside Portland in Sumner County. *From www.scv.org.*

sides of the conflict. Some guerrillas were only loosely organized and preyed indiscriminately on both the enemy and the side for which they were supposedly fighting, plundering civilians' homes and the armies' supplies.

Ancient grudges between feuding families were the impetus for some of the predations, and the Civil War was just an excuse to ramp up the action. Others, like Harper, had been commissioned to the Confederate army and were loyal to their commanders and the cause.

Harper was born in Sumner County in 1842. He was only nineteen years of age when he enlisted in the Thirtieth Tennessee Infantry, Company I in 1861. After being captured at Fort Donelson in February 1862, he was sent to Camp Butler Prison in Illinois but escaped and returned home.

Harper's knowledge of his home territory, the strategically important northern Tennessee–southern Kentucky border, attracted the attention of Colonel John Hunt Morgan, who was conducting raids designed to sabotage Union supply routes along the L&N Railroad through both states, seize munitions and supplies from captured trains and procure new recruits for his company. Morgan recruited Harper and made him a captain.

Harper's Partisan Rangers did their work efficiently and expediently, derailing trains, burning bridges and water tanks and attacking federal forage and supply details wherever they could be found. Harper had a base of operations close to the L&N Railroad and the border of the officially "neutral" Kentucky, a place known as Butler's Old Mill, with a house on the land flanking Crybaby Bridge.

On July 1, 1863, Gustavus Tafel, a lieutenant colonel commanding the 106th Regiment of the Ohio Infantry, filed this report on a skirmish with Ellis Harper at Butler's Old Mill, a few hundred yards from what is now known as Crybaby Bridge.

> *Colonel: I would respectfully submit to you the following report in regard to the ambush had by a party of your men with a force of guerrillas yesterday.... On Monday evening...information reached me that a party of guerrillas were robbing the house of Mr. Brizendine, a Union man, not far from our farthest bridge guard, about two miles from this place. I immediately ordered all the mounted men I had (number 11), under command of Lt. Berthold, to repair to the place indicated and to give pursuit if the circumstances should warrant it.* [The men rode two hours, then encountered part of the plunder lying in the road. They found their guide, who] *then conducted our party to a house where the guerrillas were known to congregate, and there they laid in wait for them. The thieves approached within sight but got wind of the presence of my men and under cover of darkness made good their escape. At daylight...the party started out again, and after a protracted search for the villains, were on their way home and some seven miles from camp, near what is called Old Butler's Mill, when they were fired upon by a force* [Harper's guerrillas] *that lay in ambush and whose numbers were estimated at from 70–120 men. Lt. Berthold fell at the first fire, shot through the heart, and the rest of the party, after a short resistance, made good their escape with the exception of one man, Charles Oferloch, private of Company E, whose horse gave out and who was overtaken and killed* [and three Union soldiers were seriously wounded]....*I had 80 suspicious characters living in the neighborhood of where the fight took place arrested, and after careful questioning, discharged three* [of the 80] *and sent the rest to Gallatin....Please find the charges against said prisoners* [attached]. *(Official Records Series I, vol. 52, part I, 67.)*

Butler's Old Mill, which was built about 1820, was located on Drake's Creek, about one hundred feet above the present-day concrete bridge on the Fowler Ford Road and was operated by Henry Sarver, a connection by marriage to O.P. Butler. This was among the very first mills in the country that ground wheat, and customers came from many miles away to get their flour, taking several days for the trip. The headquarters house of Harper, mentioned in the skirmish account, belonged to a family named Parker and still stands today, although it is dilapidated and uninhabited.

Enter Barry "Bear" Gaunt and Melvin Brazzell, the founding members of Nightstalkers Paranormal Research team based in Franklin, Kentucky. The two men have been investigating every sort of supernatural occurrence, from ghosts to Bigfoot and everything in between, for almost forty years.

"Bear" is an apt nickname for the over-six-foot-tall tree trunk of a man with a deep, throaty voice and rumbling laugh. Melvin "the Hound" is fit, wiry and quick to detect the presence of paranormal phenomena. They are night and day in their appearances, but together, they make seamless teamwork out of ferreting out spooky and even disturbing phenomena, whether it is lurking in an old hospital, hotel, historic site or private mid-century home in the suburbs. Avid history buffs, Bear and Melvin jumped at the chance to investigate phenomena with a connection to the Civil War in Sumner County. Melvin has deep roots in this part of the county; in fact, one of his ancestors was an Ellis Harper guerrilla fighter.

Game on.

"The first night at Crybaby Bridge was kind of a weird night," said Bear. "We parked on the side of the road. There was a lot of traffic, and we were surprised at the number of vehicles on the road [a two-lane country road with half-mile or more stretches between houses, most of which sit far back from the road. In addition, the country is mostly farmland consisting of many acres in each plat]. But we set up, and it was kind of an easygoing night, and then all of a sudden, there was a quick burst [on our electronic equipment indicating] a presence there. Then we hear on the recorder, 'Hello.' Then it goes silent."

Bear continued, "We see orbs of light, and then the strangest experience of the night was some sort of scream or yell that almost felt like it would be more appropriate in the jungle. I have never experienced anything like that. It sounded like a bunch of howling monkeys." A "rebel yell" somewhat garbled by time and space? "Well, yeah. I guess it could be," laughed Melvin.

"I decided to ask the 'ghost box' about the whereabouts of the old mill," he went on to say. The distinct reply: "Down the creek." Which is, of course, dead on.

Responses to questions that included the names "Ellis Harper" and that of a fellow Confederate guerrilla who was operating in Tennessee, "Champ Ferguson," got an excited response on the recorder. "We talked to the spirits with respect; we told them the history books haven't forgotten what they did in defense of their country and their kin," said Bear, "and basically, they got started murmuring, active…like they enjoyed being remembered."

"We heard heavy splashes, like men running through the creeks," he added. "Jacob and his friends heard something run through the creek just like we did, and of course, we know Ellis Harper and his crew escaped after the skirmish, through that creek."

Lucas Harper (*right*) is a descendant of Ellis Harper, a Confederate raider and Partisan Ranger. Lucas is standing with Melvin Brazzell, who also had ancestors who were in Harper's regiment. They are standing in front of the headquarters of Harper's men, just across from Crybaby Bridge. *Author's collection.*

"On our second trip, I took a night vision camera and set it up on a tripod. We got some good images," said Bear. On that second trip, the phenomena they experienced were totally different from those they experienced on the night they interacted with "Ellis Harper" and his men. "We know that a guy was killed or committed suicide in the vicinity of the bridge in the 1980s. That's where we got weird orbs. The way they moved, they weren't dust specks," said Bear. "In the tree line, we saw a white light pulsate, then here comes another one, then another moving through the trees, and we're seeing this all with a night vision camera, which picks up things that our naked eye can't pick up. The shape of this light was strange; its movement was strange. It was moving through the woods, natural and deliberate. Very intriguing," Bear recalled.

Bear remembered, "We dismantled the night vision cameras, and I was walking back to the truck and I saw a 'mist' with my naked eye, and it was 'walking' in front of me. It was a totally clear, warm summer night and…here's this mist….'Melvin, are you smoking? Did you see that?'…Melvin was not smoking, and 'yes' he saw it."

As if all that were not enough to process, right around midnight, "we hear a woman's voice talking to us on the 'ghost box,' saying, 'Let them out.'" Then the faint, thin sound of a baby crying. "There was just a whole lot going on, close together in time and in proximity," said Melvin, adding, "It's hard to separate it all out and find the origin. One thing is for sure: Ellis Harper and his men are still there, running through that creek, escaping from the skirmish with Union troops. The rest, we can only guess at."

Bear mused on the nature of paranormal phenomena and why detailed research at a site is critical before drawing conclusions of a verified haunting. "Collective consciousness can actually create a manifestation," he explained. "An example is Slenderman, and even the Black Hat Man…. Intense trauma in a location can create a shared 'illusion' in the form of an entity," Bear noted. "We just take it all in, we're not focusing in on one thing. We're observing."

"If you are in it [ghost hunting] because you think ghosts are cool and you want to go out every Friday night to get scared and hope for a TV show, you won't succeed. You must do research, get background on the property. It's an investigation," Bear concluded. "The history here confirms what we heard and experienced."

5

Glowing Skulls and Robbers' Plunder

Myths cast spells that cannot be broken by facts.
—*Andrew Lawler*

Tennessee has 8,600 known caves—more than any other state. In fact, 20 percent of all caves in the United States are found in Tennessee, and Sumner County boasts 42. The Cumberland Plateau has given birth to these compelling natural formations, and caves are found at the bottom of the county's numerous sinkholes and on bluffs at the head of a spring. Native tribes used them as temporary shelter, as did the first White settlers in the area and seasonal hunters and trappers known as long hunters.

In April 1907, a man told a bizarre and somewhat unbelievable story to the *Owensburg* (KY) *Messenger-Inquirer*. It seems he was part of a fishing party that, in 1888, stumbled on what is known as Robbers Cave, or the Cave of Horrors, about five miles from Gallatin on a high bluff overlooking the Cumberland River. The cave had been so named because it was thought to be a place where river pirates many years before had taken their captives and relieved them of their valuables, killed them and left their bodies to rot in the cave.

A violent storm had interrupted the men's fishing, and they sought refuge in the cave, but the narrator of this story had been wise enough to bring along a candle and matches in his coat pocket. After entering the cave through a very tight crawl space, the men were astonished to see "the ground literally covered with these unsightly objects [human skulls], all seeming to wear a fiendish smile."

> *Advancing, awe-stricken, to near the center of the chamber, a large wooden box, or chest met our gaze.... We could see what appeared to be a glittering gold color* [inside the box].... *We made a rush for the box.... There was a bright flash of lightning, followed by a deafening report, and then all was dark—my candle was extinguished. Spellbound, I could move neither hand nor foot, when suddenly, as if by magic, the skulls lying at our feet lighted up with a pale green light, the sightless eyes and grinning teeth making a horrible spectacle. Turning my eyes to where the chest stood, my eyes fell upon the dim outline of an old man with* [a] *flowing white* [haired] *beard seated on the chest. Slowly...he pointed a long, bony finger toward the entrance, where we had come and then vanished.*

The narrator reported that a hasty retreat was made by all.

After returning home, the men's retelling of their thrilling experience made for a mad dash by "those who were brave and 'not afraid of anything,'" who "visited the place" and came back with the same spine-chilling tale as the initial explorers—and no gold treasure.

All further attempts at retrieving the mysterious box that glinted of gold failed, according to the narrator.

This suspiciously tall tale does have some factual basis, as caves in the area have been used to store plunder.

On June 3, 1882, the *Clarksville* (TN) *Weekly Chronicle* reported a spectacular find, discovered by D.K. Spillers and Major W.S. Munday while they were exploring a cave on the farm of Colonel Jas Alexander in Gallatin.

> [For] *the last five years, the cave has been the rendezvous of the James brothers gang of outlaws....* [Spillers and Munday] *discovered a large, flat rock in one of the chambers and, thinking that some of the secrets of the gang might be hidden away under it, removed it with great difficulty when, to their utter astonishment, a large cast iron sugar kettle filled with specie and jewels of various kinds met their view.*
>
> *They could hardly believe their senses but finally managed to examine the treasure and found that there was over $40,000 in specie besides numerous gold watches, rings, diamonds and other jewelry of great value.*

The James Gang, the famed post–Civil War outlaws, hid much of their plunder in the caves of Sumner County. They once purchased a horse from the Rosemont Thoroughbred farm in Gallatin. *Pictured, left to right*: Frank and Jesse. *From.www.wikimedia.org.*

Major Monday guarded the great treasure while Mr. Spillers, hastening to Gallatin and securing his horse and wagon, returned as speedily as possible to the cave.

They placed the kettle and contents in the wagon and drove rapidly to Gallatin and, at once, deposited the treasure in the vaults of the Sumner Deposit Company. The greatest excitement prevails, and the Sumner guards have been ordered to the cave to prevent a hungry horde of curiosity hunters and treasure seekers from completely ransacking it. This is the second lot of valuables found in the cave since the death of Jesse James. Thousands of visitors have been denied admission by Colonel Alexander, and it is by strenuous efforts that any portion of its contents are spared from seekers of mementos of the great bandits. A considerable portion of the jewelry is in the original boxes as they left the jewelers and contain the addresses of many jewelers throughout the West and also a few in the East. Colonel Alexander has already sent a great many of the former lot to several parties in various portions of the United States. Further explorations will be made at once as it is thought other valuables may still be hidden in the cave.

Cave lore is firmly entrenched in Gallatin with the presence of Alexander's Caves, later known as Lackey's Caves when the property changed hands, according to local historian Jerry Lumpkins.

The most popular access to the cave, for many years, was in the vicinity of Lock Four Road, not far from present-day Rucker-Stewart Middle School. For over fifty years, this entrance has been filled in, and a subdivision was built on it. But until that time, it was a popular spot for kids to play.

In the early 1960s, Barry Draper was a ten-year-old kid ripe for adventure and exploration, especially when school was out for the summer. "We had no air conditioning back then. On a hot summer day, we neighborhood kids would pack a lunch and go where it was cool: the caves," said Draper. "As a small kid, it was no big deal to wiggle in the small hole to access the cave, but as a middle-schooler it was a little tougher. Nevertheless, it was worth it to see actual stalactites and stalagmites in a spacious cavern, as well as a creek running through the cave.…There were no houses there; it was a big field with a farm."

"We had always heard a story about a settler family back in the day that had a house on the property close to Town Creek. One day, Indians attacked, the husband was killed and the rest of the family ran to the caves, never to be seen again.…Well, of course the legend arose that you could hear the voices of the wife and kids calling out from the depths of the cave if you listen really hard," Draper said. "Is it imagination? We heard things in that cave, but who knows?"

"It's no 'tall tale' that the caves were used by Confederates to escape detection by occupying Union forces during the Civil War," said Jerry Lumpkins. "There are small entrances to the caves in many a backyard in the vicinity of the Sumner County Museum and the Methodist Church."

It is here that imagination and local legend start to run amok. Some say Lackey's Caves run all under the public square, out to Fairvue Plantation, under Walmart and everywhere in between. Others say they found an entrance at the First Baptist Church, started exploring and came up several miles north of town—or started at Lock 4 and ended up on College Street.

Lumpkins said it's no legend that "behind the Presbyterian church on Main Street, the cave water used to run out, all the way to the cemetery. Some of those nearby houses have access to the cave....There's no telling how many entrances and outlets there are."

"On Red River Road, right by Colonel Elliott's old home, caves were explored in the early 1900s," said Lumpkins. And it "had to be pretty deep in parts, because the explorers dropped their buckets down in the water in the cave and came up with not only water but with an eyeless fish—it had eye sockets but no eyes, like one of the rare cavefish first discovered at Mammoth Cave. The find at Gallatin is reputed to be the farthest south in the United States that the fish has been seen." The first cavefish recognized in the scientific literature was the Northern Cavefish (*Amblyopsis spelaea*), which was identified in 1842 in Kentucky. This fish was known to Darwin, who wrote in *The Origin* about their eyeless condition, an adaptation to the lack of light in caves.

Lumpkins said the construction of the Highway 109 Bypass probably took out the last of the easily accessible entrances to Lackey's Cave.

Caves are prevalent throughout the area, and some were used to hide Confederate soldiers and their supplies from patrolling Union occupational forces during the Civil War.

Judy Newman lives in Castalian Springs in a house that was built in the 1880s. Caves that legend says were used by Confederate guerrillas are in the vicinity of her home. She experiences unexplained noises, her cat plays with something she cannot see and she has electrical appliance disruptions. After moving into the home, while taking photographs of its original woodwork to show to a friend in California, Newman took a photograph that showed a woman and a little boy, both clothed in attire from long ago, reflected in the mirror of her bedroom. "I was frightened at first, but that night, I just announced to the room, 'Please don't show yourself or frighten me,'" Newman said. She has not seen an apparition since, although disturbances, such as a heavy fireplace grate flying across the room during a family gathering, have occurred.

6

The Haunted Past of Log Structures

Everyone from around here has some dim family memory or tradition of the old home place with its spring branch, rocky pastures, creek bottom land, saddle horses, stone fences and grandparents who farmed.

The Cumberland Gap was our birth canal, and we lost touch with the folks left behind two centuries ago in the Carolinas and Virginia. We are and always have been a distinct culture. We are Middle Tennesseans.

—*Bill Puryear*

Spring comes in waves of color and bouts of capricious weather in Middle Tennessee. The undulating fields display wildflowers that are first yellow, then purple and finally white, carpeting the pastures that will turn emerald green in the summer months after vigorous storms—often with deadly tornadoes—punctuate the spring months. Here and there on hillsides and by rippling creeks, log homes dot the landscape of Tennessee—from the original, settler-built structures that started out as simple two-room dogtrots to twenty-first-century country music celebrity mansions that have been reproduced to look like the log homes of yore but with every modern comfort and amenity.

When this land was being settled by White families in the late 1700s, it appeared to have never been broken by cultivation and was covered in thick canebrakes, with forest trees of mammoth size. This is hard to picture, considering the rolling fertile fields and expanses of grazing land that exist there today. More than 1,500 land grants were issued in the Cumberland Settlement, as Middle Tennessee was then known.

Wynnewood is an 1828 log structure that was built by Alfred Wynne as an inn for travelers. During the early 1800s, it had a horseracing track that attracted visitors such as Andrew Jackson. *Author's collection.*

Sumner County has numerous log structures of distinction, and Wynnewood is a prime example. The handsome log inn was erected in 1828 by A.R. Wynne, William Cage and Stephen Roberts on land that was owned by Wynne's wife, Almira Winchester Wynne. It was to serve as a stagecoach inn and mineral springs resort. A log cabin attached to the rear of the inn was erected by Isaac Bledsoe between 1772 and 1780, when he came to this area as a long hunter. In 1834, Wynne purchased the interest of his two partners. He and his family moved into the inn and resided there until his death in 1893. The ownership of Wynnewood remained in the family until 1971, when George Winchester Wynne, the grandson of the builder, conveyed it to the State of Tennessee for its preservation as a historic site.

A.R. Wynne received guests at Wynnewood throughout his lifetime. By the 1840s, he had built a row of cottages on the lawn east of the inn and set up a racecourse near Lick Creek. Most guests were attracted by the medicinal qualities of the mineral waters, but one frequent visitor, Andrew Jackson, was attracted by the racecourse, and he usually brought a favorite Thoroughbred to run against one of Wynne's horses. During the Civil War, Wynnewood was not disturbed, although both the Union and Confederate armies passed by its front doors as they hastened along the road between engagements at

The Bridal House is a log structure that was built in the early 1800s as a wedding present from Moore Carter Cotton for his only daughter, Elizabeth Frances "Betsy" Cotton. It is located on State Highway 25 in Cottontown. *Author's collection.*

Hartsville and Gallatin. During the years of the Union army's occupation, there was a fortified camp complete with earthworks located on Wynne's property, about one half mile southwest of the inn.

In Cottontown, the Bridal House was believed to have been built in 1819 by Moore Carter Cotton for his only daughter, Elizabeth Frances "Betsy" Cotton, as a bridal gift for her marriage to Richard Hobdy, Cotton's apprentice. Cotton wanted her to reside within earshot of the Cotton mansion. He was a prosperous blacksmith who lived in the only brick house for miles around.

Four yoke of oxen brought the largest poplar logs ever seen in that area down the "Bug Hollow Trail," which runs alongside Station Camp Creek. A man named Brigham from Ziegler's Station was commissioned to hew the logs into building shape. Fifteen months later, the Bridal House was move-in ready. The house is now owned by Sumner County and has been restored, after almost two hundred years of use by various owners. There was a time when it was covered in clapboard, which eventually deteriorated and hung in sad sheets until a new owner took the clapboard down and rehabbed the logs.

New Moon Farm

When Emily Greer Tuttle's family bought the two-story home they named New Moon Farm, it was 1957, and the sturdy, hand-hewn log structure was already 160 years old—almost older than the State of Tennessee itself—and had passed through many hands.

Children who grow up on the farms that were established on land grants following the American Revolution are typically blithely unaware of the significance of their land and its survival through generations of Native attacks, the Civil War, droughts, economic depressions and the hazards of everyday existence. Farm kids like the Tuttle children enjoyed the freedom of wandering across acres and acres of farmland, woods, ponds and caves, often finding arrowheads. Emily said, "We certainly had heard stories of early settlers killed and scalped in their own front yards, which terrified me as a child."

"We were aware that our farm was supposed to have some sort of buried treasure," said Susan Dalton, Emily Tuttle's sister, "because people used to come with metal detectors and roam around looking for things. They never found anything, but our property was a 'rural,' rather than 'urban' legend because of a rumor that survived generations regarding buried coins or valuables."

If hundreds of dolls, which belonged to the Tuttle sisters' mother, creep you out, New Moon Farm is not for you, as your imagination will quickly take over. But it is not the "doll room" that is haunted. "We believe the main source of the paranormal activity here is the furniture that belonged to Elmer Ellsworth Robb, our great-grandfather who never lived here, but his bed, rocking chair and several other pieces of his furniture have been here for years," said Emily, "throughout our childhoods."

Elmer Ellsworth Robb was, plainly, "a carpetbagger," according to Susan, who added that he was named after the Union general who took down a Confederate flag in Alexandria, Virginia, and got shot for his efforts, which made him a hero to the Yankees. Robb came from Ohio to Madison, Tennessee, after the Civil War, and as a northern Republican, he had all the right connections to become postmaster, schoolteacher and general store proprietor in the Reconstruction-era South. "He married his pupil Almira Wingo. He was twenty-four and she was fourteen," said Susan.

The "haunted room" with Robb's furniture and portrait is "spooky," according to both Susan and Emily. "Some family members refused to sleep in that room, and all had the same experience if they did—what can only be

Above: New Moon Farm is and always has been a family home. "It has always had a dog," said Emily Tuttle, who is pictured (*left*) with her sister Susan Dalton and Smedley. The sisters grew up at the farm. *Author's collection.*

Right: Susan Dalton says the eyes of their great-grandfather Elmer Robb follow visitors about the bedroom where his furniture is located. *Author's collection.*

Emily Tuttle (*left*) and sister Susan Dalton maintain a working farm where they grew up in Cottontown. The land-grant farm has been in the possession of many families over the years and dates to the late 1700s. *Author's collection.*

described as a 'clammy lightness,' like a wet sheet would pass over them in the night; the rocking chair rocked on its own....Elmer Robb dominates that one room, there's no question," said Susan. "He watches."

"I always had anxiety about the second story of the house growing up," reported Susan. "'It' stayed upstairs. The presence was very vivid, and I sensed it was female and protective but not harmful in any way."

"Once, it did come down," said Susan. "I was sleeping downstairs, and suddenly, it was there. I could feel pressure on my face; I felt it was hovering over me, extremely close, and the presence at that range seemed to go on forever. I knew I had finally come face to face with it. And weirdly, it seemed like the entity was trying to make peace. After that experience, I felt reconciled to the presence and no longer afraid."

HANCOCK HOUSE

Just like Wynnewood, Hancock House was built for travelers as a stagecoach stop through the Thoroughbred horse country of Sumner County on the way to conduct commerce and government in Nashville, Memphis and New Orleans. The two-story log structure's current owners, Roberta and Carl Hancock, raised a family there, beginning in the 1970s, and then turned the spacious log home into a bed-and-breakfast and a venue for weddings and other social gatherings in 1990.

Prior to the home's ownership by the Hancocks, it was, for years, owned by the colorful and vivacious Mary Felice Ferrell, who was sadly killed instantly in a car accident in front of the house in the late 1970s. "I had visited Miss Mary Felice there as a child, and I told her, 'I'm going to live here someday,'" said Roberta. When the home became available, Roberta told husband Carl, "I really want this house." To which Carl replied, looking at the enormity and the challenge of a 150-year-old structure, "It will kill me."

Nonetheless, the couple bought the home, raised a family there and now operate a successful business there, where Southern grace and fortitude keep alive the traditions of entertaining guests as if they were family, attending to the comforts of each guest and personally doing all the shopping and cooking.

Raven-haired and petite, with arresting, dark eyes and a quick but soft southern accent, the energetic Roberta Hancock could give Scarlett O'Hara a run for her money in tenacity and grace under pressure. A fire started by lightning destroyed the Hancocks' kitchen the night prior to a wedding they were hired to cater. But it did not slow Roberta down one bit. "We moved everything that had to be prepped for the wedding to the cabin adjacent to the big house and carried on," she said.

Carl is tall, white-haired and soft-spoken, with a dry wit and the bearing of a classic southern gentleman. Like Roberta, he has the uncanny ability to make friends out of strangers in a very short period, and he shares equally in the food preparation.

Since it is located in Sumner County, "Of course Hancock House is haunted," said Roberta. "The paranormal presence has been with me from the very first day I ever visited as a child," and it carries through the daily life and activities in the busy house. "I never say anything to the guests ahead of time about the spirit activity. I just wait until they come down for breakfast, then someone will timidly say, 'Um, did you know your house is haunted?'" laughed Roberta. "Although, not everyone who stays here is 'sensitive' to the activity."

As the Hancock children, Catherine and Hampton, grew from toddlers to young adults in the historic structure, they, too, experienced many ghostly sightings, and Roberta said Hampton could describe, in "great detail," the

Above: Hancock House, a popular bed-and-breakfast that has been the scene of many weddings, bridal showers and festive dinners, was built as a stagecoach inn for travelers going to and from Nashville and points farther south. It was built around 1832. *Author's collection.*

Left: Strangers leave as friends when they visit Hancock House Bed and Breakfast. The once-private home of Carl and Roberta Hancock not only hosts overnight visitors in its antique-appointed bedrooms, but its dining and reception areas have been the scene of weddings and graduation parties, as well as intimate dinners, for more than thirty years. *Author's collection.*

clothing of a young Native boy who played with him in the woods behind the house. "He was no imaginary friend," she said. "His presence lasted too many years, and Hampton had such details regarding him that we believe he was a spirit."

Both Roberta and Catherine saw the spectral outlines of three women in clothing from the mid-1800s standing at the foot of the stairs on several occasions. Women can be heard talking, laughing and bustling about the house on many nights, but they cannot be found. Footsteps go up and down the staircase, most often from the dining room, up the short staircase, to the guest rooms. Doors are heard opening and closing. "We have had wedding guests take photos of the bridal party, and when they are developed, a ghostly image would appear, standing right there as if part of the group."

Most notably and humorously, one of the Hancocks' repeat guests, who always swore he was a total skeptic when it came to the paranormal, had the most profound experience in the house. "This couple would come stay with us about three to four times a year, and the man was a scientific-minded person. In fact, he was an engineer of some kind, perhaps for the space program," said Roberta.

Roberta Hancock (*left*) once saw three ghostly women at the foot of the stairs walk slowly by. They were dressed in the mid-1800s style. Her husband, Carl (*right*), is an "open-minded skeptic." *Author's collection.*

One of Mary Felice Farrell's boarders back in the 1940s was a man who was studying to be a doctor. This regular visitor—the skeptic—had a bad bout of indigestion one night from eating too much at a local restaurant.

The following morning, when he came down to breakfast, he said, "Where is the doctor who is staying here? I woke up with this man in a white coat and a thermometer in his hand and one hand on my head. I want to thank him for being so kind."

Well, of course, there was no doctor staying here that night. This very literal engineer just couldn't wrap his head around it.

Visitors Crystal Stallings Jump and Renee Sullivan stayed in a room with an adjoining bath. "Someone kept tapping on the door of the bathroom when I was taking a morning shower," said Crystal. "I thought it was Renee, but she was on the opposite side of the suite, in the small sitting area between rooms, doing paperwork on her computer tablet. This happened twice during our stay," said Crystal.

Like Rosemont, Hancock House is a home that has seen many guests come through its doors over the span of almost two hundred years. And like so many ancestral places in Sumner County that echo the cheer and conviviality of bygone days of prosperity, opulent gatherings and throngs of enthusiastic visitors, Hancock House's resident spirits are just wanting to be part of the delight of entertaining travelers, newcomers and old friends.

7

A Ghostly Pastor and Ghosts by the Railroad Tracks

Sumner County historian, educator, author and chronicler of the area's Black history and heritage Velma Brinkley remembers a day when an excited fellow church parishioner called her to say her son had just taken a photograph of a ghost on the railroad track by Gray Street in Gallatin. Indeed, Brinkley and several church members viewed the image on the church member's son's cellphone, and to their astonishment, not only was there a picture of a shadowy figure but its features were clearly distinguishable as those of one of the earliest pastors of First Baptist Church on Winchester Street, Reverend Peter Vertrees.

Regina Davis also viewed the photograph directly on the phone and identified the man as Vertrees. She commented, "It looked like he was wearing a uniform—an old Civil War uniform."

As is mentioned in the chapters on the Civil War in Sumner County, the L&N Railroad figures prominently in the area's history as a supply route for Civil War troops; therefore, it was a point of contention for the warring North and South. It was a major avenue of interstate commerce for a developing country, replacing the cumbersome overland travel on primitive roads and languorous water routes.

It is on the tracks just north of Gallatin's public square that one of the town's most illustrious citizens has been seen—and photographed. Peter Vertrees came from humble beginnings in rural Kentucky. He was the son of a young White woman and a mulatto preacher, which, in 1840, was a pedigree not likely to lead to anything other than life as an enslaved

Peter Vertrees, a cook, assistant surgeon and infantryman of the Sixth Kentucky CSA and founding pastor of almost sixty Sumner County churches, has been seen along the railroad tracks in Gallatin. *From www.EdmondsonVets.com.*

person. But at the time of his death in 1921, Vertrees's achievements included being a scholar, educator, Baptist minister, musician and Confederate veteran.

Born in Edmonson County, Kentucky, to the great-grand-niece of American patriot Patrick Henry, Peter's young mother gave him over to indentured servitude at the age of five. Fortuitously, his master was Jacob Vertrees, who reared his own illegitimate grandson and treated him as a free member of the family.

When the Civil War broke out, Kentucky was deeply divided, and young men rushed to sign up on both sides of the conflict. Despite having been raised as a free man, Peter Vertrees's skin color prevented him from enlisting in the Confederate army to serve alongside the male members of his family who had enthusiastically declared their loyalty to the South after the Confederate victory at Manassas in 1861. But Peter's uncle Dr. John Luther Vertrees had a plan: he would take Peter with him as an assistant and cook while he served as a surgeon for the troops.

Even during the early days of training and drilling, there was no end to the diseases and illnesses experienced by the troops due to the unsanitary conditions of camp life, the shortage of decent food and the close quarters that were breeding grounds for fevers and ailments. Dr. John and Peter tended the men of the Sixth Kentucky with diligence and care until their health improved and they were fit for fighting. It was "out of the frying pan into the fire," as the Sixth Kentucky braved the bloody 1862 Battle of Shiloh, earning the reputation as one of the hardest-fighting units of the Confederate army.

Peter Vertrees spent his army life behind the lines of battle, but he would see the grim results of warfare. In the Atlanta campaign alone, the Kentuckians would see 1,860 wounded men, and many of them were fatally wounded. At Shiloh, Dr. Vertrees and his orderlies, including Peter Vertrees, treated both wounded southerners and Yankees. Many of the northerners had never seen a Black man until they were ministered to by Peter Vertrees.

Vicksburg followed the horrors of Shiloh, and Peter Vertrees would recall in later life that the troops were forced to eat horsemeat because the beef and pork had given out. As a cook, Peter was always on the lookout for ways to enhance the meager menu of the troops. "One day I thought about how a nice mess of fresh river fish would be, so I got on a gray horse and went down to the Mississippi River to fish. I had not been there long when I heard a humming sound over my head….A federal gunboat [was leaning to one side], and smoke rose from it." Peter realized the "humming" had been the sound of bullets whizzing over his head. Though he was armed with a pistol (many historians have adamantly refused to believe any Black man accompanying Confederate troops would be allowed a firearm), Peter quickly decided, "I like fish, but I like life better," and gave up the idea of a fresh-caught meal.

Vertrees and his uncle Dr. John Vertrees endured the entire war and received their parole in Dalton, Georgia, in May 1865. Later, Peter Vertrees would say, "I stayed at my post until the end."

Devotion to a cause would be the hallmark of Vertrees's life from that day forward, and he dedicated himself to establishing churches and charity organizations in Sumner County. "I went into the communities where there was no church and organized one," Vertrees has said. Even when there were not enough interested persons in a community, Vertrees would "borrow" church members from another location, hold a religious service and post "Will Malone, who was a sinner, but pious [who] would stand guard with his shotgun for fear of an attack on Reverend Vertrees' life, [for the] wicked men would be off a short distance drinking and gambling, cursing and dancing. The gamblers and drunkards heard the word of God and were converted and baptized."

In 1874, Vertrees took over the duties of the pastor at First Baptist Church on Winchester Street in Gallatin, which was then housed in a little log house. That little log house was replaced by a white frame church and then a building that was made from bricks purchased cheaply from the old penitentiary in Nashville.

Pastor Vertrees left his earthly duties in 1926, leaving the church in the hands of Dr. J.N. Rucker. The number of churches established in Sumner County by Peter Vertrees or guided by his hand is almost too large to count.

First Baptist has been in the same location in Gallatin on Winchester Street since 1865 and continues to expand its enthusiastic and committed congregation.

But there is a twist to the story of the cellphone photograph that so clearly depicts Peter Vertrees: "Although a photo could be taken and the photo could be viewed, the phone was totally without power," said Brinkley—both when the photograph was taken and when it was shown to various people. And why would Vertrees appear on the railroad tracks?

The railroad tracks in that vicinity have a history of spectral sightings. Emma Malone said:

> *We lived over near Blythe Street, and I would walk to Terry's Market as a child. One night, by the railroad tracks, I saw a man standing there, by the cemetery, close to the old radio station. This man had died a few years before; I knew him—my family knew him.*
>
> *I just stood there. It was unmistakable that it was him. He had this one "funny" eye, and he was wearing this suit that he always wore. My friend was walking a little ahead of me, and I called to her, then turned back, and the man was gone.*

Others along that same street have reported a man standing by the railroad tracks who disappears when a train passes by.

8

GHOSTS AND CRYPTIDS IN THE MOUNT OLIVET COMMUNITY

The paranormal is very alive and well and always has been in the Mount Olivet African American community.
—Velma Brinkley

Some of the paranormal activity in the Mount Olivet community is so pervasive and so frightening that folks don't even want to talk about it for fear that it will "stir up the entities."

Historically, the Mount Olivet community, prior to becoming surrounded by tract homes and the retail development of Nashville's bedroom community of Hendersonville, has comprised about fifteen families who farmed for themselves and "tended White peoples' farms" well into the late 1900s, according to Mattie Shaw, whose roots there go back many generations. "We grew what we ate, and we did a lot of canning," Shaw noted.

Growing up there in the 1940s, "we walked everywhere—to school and to church—and we were always careful to get back home before dark," Shaw remembered. But she also recalled traveling in a buggy at times. "We had chickens; we had pigs. It was quite an art to dress a chicken and stretch a pot," said Shaw, remembering that it was much admired for a housewife to use one chicken to make three different dishes. "There were only two cars in the whole community, so we walked in groups to church and community events. Now, nobody walks. There are just so many cars" on the 1.7 miles that comprise Mount Olivet Road, said Shaw.

"Grown-ups didn't talk too much about ghosts and such around the children," said Shaw. "I remember my daddy talking some about such things that would happen after people would pass. I do remember the tradition when someone would die, a room in a house would be cleaned out, and the deceased would be laid out and a chair or two placed in the room. People came in groups all night long to pray, bring food and visit," reminisced Shaw, whose own mother died when she was only six years old.

"There was one funny story about a man in the community who had died. He was a humpbacked man, and they had to strap him firmly into the casket. During the wake, the straps broke, and the man sat straight up," Shaw laughed. "You know that everyone emptied out of there mighty fast."

One night, while walking home in a group, Mattie and her companions saw the apparition of a little girl near the cemetery. When the group told their parents about it, their elders admitted that others in the community had seen the child, who was believed to be Mattie's cousin who had died at a very young age. She appeared many times "all dressed up, like the day she was buried."

"They would see the child going toward the church and go try to get a closer look. They would then find nobody," Mattie said. "My mama's sister saw her, and from time to time, so would others."

"At dark, there were 'hotspots'"—not the cold spots normally associated with paranormal activity. "It would all of a sudden be oven-hot, and somebody would scream 'haints,' and we'd run." The community began to associate the hotspots with ghostly activity on that strip of road. "We'd hear footsteps behind us. If we sped up, those footsteps would speed up."

But stranger than the hot spots and ghostly child was the occasional sighting of a bird so enormous that its wingspan went from one side of the road to the other. "My brother-in-law was traveling in his truck one night, and a bird of such enormity that he said he could not see its wings from tip to tip, only the underside of its belly as it hovered over the hood of his truck, suddenly appeared," Mattie reported. "My brother-in-law didn't know whether to speed up, go backward or forward. The bird had 'sailed' not flapped, he told us, and when he finally did decide to move forward and the bird disengaged from his hood, he looked back to see where it was, and it had disappeared as quickly as it had come and was nowhere in sight."

"Oh, yes, it is strange down there in that area," between Longhollow Pike and the Mount Olivet Road, said Emma Malone. "It's a major thoroughfare now, but before Longhollow was widened, it was a rural road, with trees on each side that could touch each other, making a kind of tunnel," said

Malone. "On that same road, we once saw a large white object fly over our car. It was too big to be a bird; it was huge, the size of a person. It was just 'flapping'—that's the only way I know to describe it—a huge flapping white thing, and it flew right to the cemetery," said Malone.

By tribal law, traditional Cherokee tales and stories are only told to other members of the tribe. These stories often feature animals, birds, supernatural beings and daring exploits of tribesmen and women. The legend of the *tlanuwa* or the great mythic hawk is a Cherokee version of the Thunderbird myth found in mostly southwestern cultures. Tlanuwa are huge, cave-dwelling raptors that will search for prey by flying up and down riverbanks. Legend says they are large enough to carry off animals and small children. Could the tlanuwa still be seen in the area, known to have been part of Cherokee tribal lands? Certainly, the numerous caves in the area could be the lairs of these creatures, just as tradition holds.

Malone also remembered a persistent occurrence on that same lonely road. "On some nights, there would be an old car on that road, a car that you could not pass" if you found yourself travelling behind it—at least not until the car got past the cemetery that was just before what is now Longhollow Baptist Church. "Then that car would disappear."

9

Grave Robbers and Body Snatchers

Tallest Man in the World

The birth of John William "Bud" Rogan in 1868 challenged the status quo of a burgeoning medical scholarly community. His physical development appeared to be normal until he noticeably continued growing in stature beyond his teenage period.

John William "Bud" Rogan was recorded in the *Guinness Book of World Records* as the second-tallest person in history (until he was surpassed in height by Robert Wadlow, who was just centimeters short of being nine feet tall, in 1940). Born in Sumner County, the son of a formerly enslaved man, Bud was the fourth of twelve children.

Bud began to grow very rapidly at the age of thirteen. It was soon discovered by local physicians that he was fast becoming a giant and was suffering from ankylosis, or a rigidity of the knee and hip joints, a condition often found in cases of gigantism. By 1882, he could not stand or walk. Despite his debilitating condition, Bud developed a very lucrative business by meeting all trains at the depot and selling postcards that depicted him. To facilitate his mobility, he rode in a small four-wheeled wagon that was built to his specifications and was pulled by a span of goats.

Rogan's talents extended to pen and pencil drawings, and a few were published in newspapers. He declined all offers to join carnivals and sideshows.

"Bud" Rogan, the second-tallest man in the world, according to the *Guinness Book of World Records*, was known as the goat man. His goat cart pulled him around town, as his medical condition made it impossible for him to walk. Rogan made his living selling postcards depicting himself. Several of his drawings were published in newspapers around the country. He refused to be part of circuses or tent shows. *From r/OldSchoolCool, www.reddit.com.*

Bud was thoroughly examined in 1898 by Dr. E.F. Hickman, assisted by Dr. William Nicholas Lackey. At that time, he measured eight feet, six inches tall and often appeared in newspapers, in which he was referred to as the "negro giant."

He was always the center of attention, often noted for his deep voice and playful attitude.

Rogan died at the age of thirty-seven on September 12, 1905, due to complications from his ankylosis. According to the *Guinness Book of Records*, Rogan's hands measured 11.5 inches (29 centimeters) in length, and his feet measured 13.7 inches (35 centimeters) in length. He grew to be 8 feet, 9 inches (2.67 meters) tall but weighed only 205 pounds (93 kilograms). When he died in 1905, his family buried him in a secret place, covering his grave with railroad crossties and several feet of concrete to prevent resourceful doctors from robbing the grave. In medical journals, he is referred to only by his initials.

His family was circumspect in hiding his gravesite from prying eyes and medical students, as Bud Rogan's death occurred during the heyday of medical students robbing graves of their cadavers to use them in their rapidly developing medical research. It was a double-edged sword, as the cadavers provided the necessary means to advance medical science, but the legal system had not yet caught up with passing laws to deter the practice.

A Grisly Business

In the 1500s, as medical science was in its infancy, the hangman provided most of the human cadavers used for studying, and the religious attitudes of the time and the politics and beliefs of Henry VIII were part of the mix of oddities surrounding the business of what came to be known as body snatching.

Carol and Frank Jarboe are living historians based in Kentucky, just a few miles north of Sumner County, who portray "resurrectionists," or body snatchers, for cemetery tours and other history-oriented events. In the United States in the 1800s, "the resurrection men, as they were called, looked for cemeteries with fresh graves that were not being watched and graves of paupers, Blacks and the lower class, usually in isolated areas," said Carol.

"A religious belief originating in the 1500s was that the soul of any dead body that was cut on, cut up or dissected was doomed to wander the earth forever," said Carol. "Henry VIII of England specifically ordered murderers to be cut up or dissected to keep them from entering heaven," she added. Before long, however, doctors found that criminals' corpses could not meet the demand of medical schools.

In the 1800s, medical faculties often had trouble finding enough bodies for their students to dissect in classrooms, but families were reluctant to donate the bodies of their loved ones to science. Tragically, the bodies that medical instructors typically obtained came from the most victimized and outcast members of society. When available, the corpses for the dissecting room were found in poorhouses, jails and mental asylums for the simple reason that those who died there had often been abandoned by their families.

The largest number of bodies dissected by medical students in the United States from the 1800s into the 1930s were those of Black people. A large number of those who were paid or encouraged to do the grave robbing were also Black. "African Americans often served as medical assistants to White students, as many turn-of-the-century photographs of dissections show, but rarely became doctors then," said Stephen Taylor in a blog.

It is ironic, therefore, that the tallest Black man in history, Rogan, as well as one of the most prolific body snatchers in history, Rufus Cantrell, also a Black man, should hail from Gallatin. In the late 1800s, Cantrell moved north with his family and settled in Indianapolis. "Cantrell was prosecuted for extensive grave-robbing in 1903. When pressed, and perhaps enjoying the media attention, [he took] investigators around cemeteries all over the city where he and his 'gang' had removed corpses," wrote Taylor.

Dawn Mitchell, in an article in the *Indianapolis Star*, stated:

> *When police arrested Rufus Cantrell on suspicion of grave robbing in 1901, they had no idea the scope of the operation. Newspaper accounts referred to Cantrell as "The King of the Ghouls," a grave-robbing syndicate that emptied graves across Indianapolis for the purpose of selling them to medical colleges. Cantrell spilled the beans on every operation and rode with police around the city, pointing out more than 100 empty graves. He even led them to the basements of several medical colleges and implicated the doctors who ran the institutions. Cantrell also helped police close investigations of several high-profile missing persons cases—admitting their bodies were taken to medical colleges and then disposed of.*
>
> *Medical students needed the hands-on study of human anatomy, yet there were no legal ways for medical schools to procure cadavers for dissections. Students would take matters into their own hands and steal corpses, but in the late 1890s, the practice of stealing corpses by unscrupulous individuals was big business—and business was booming.*
>
> *They were called night ghouls, body snatchers and resurrectionists.*
>
> *There were two rules for grave robbing—wait until the mourners had left the cemetery, and never allow a subject to lie in its grave overnight.*
>
> *Early grave robbing was sloppy, careless, and attracted attention. Grave robbers then changed their tactics and placed the clothes back in the grave. Jewels and keepsakes were a bonus, but they had to be careful not to sell them locally, for fear of the pieces being recognized.*
>
> *Body snatching was a three-man operation: one to drive the carriage and two to remove the remains. It was customary to open the grave and pull the corpse out with an iron hook placed under the chin. The body was stripped naked and wrapped in heavy cloth, leaving the shrouds and clothes behind. The grave was restored, bodies delivered, and the robbers paid $15–$30 for an hour's work.*

Part of the mystery and spookiness of any cemetery comes from the belief that souls of the dead who were buried there wander and manifest when the sun goes down, whether or not their bodies have any parts missing.

Family cemeteries, with graves going back to the late 1700s, are tucked here and there about Sumner County. Douglass Cemetery in the Salem Community is one such burial ground. James Douglass, a Revolutionary War veteran, was the recipient of a land grant in what was then part of North Carolina. He brought his family to Middle Tennessee in the late 1700s, and his two brothers soon followed. They acquired another large portion of land, and soon, the Douglasses were an expanding family of hardworking settlers. Native depredations were still numerous enough that the Douglasses built their own fort.

Necessarily, a family cemetery was established; the sixty-foot-by-sixty-foot piece of land was enclosed by heavy rocks, drilled so that pig iron fencing could be inserted into the holes. Over the years, the cemetery fell into great disrepair. Cattle from adjacent land trampled the fencing; kids, intrigued by the aboveground crypts that held the remains of Douglasses long departed, had played among the graves and inflicted small damages that added up over the decades.

"Teenagers in the '50s and '60s used to park at night on the road at the cemetery and call 'Bay Raven! Bay Raven!' Somehow, some legend grew up that the cemetery was haunted. This was egged on by adults who added on to the stories with tales of a half-man, half-woman named Bay Raven," said Margaret Hunter, a longtime Salem community resident who worked with Salem community leaders to restore the cemetery before her death in 2016.

Civil War reenactors prepare to fire a cannon during Memorial Day celebrations at Gallatin City Cemetery. *Author's collection.*

Ghost hunters visit Gallatin City Cemetery, where a pervasive sulfur smell, rumored to indicate demons, hangs in the air on some nights—and an occasional light orb may float by.

Could grave robbing and body snatching be the reason some of the spirits that frequent cemeteries are restless?

The City of Gallatin is currently renovating portions of the Gallatin City Cemetery, and archeological studies are being done to locate the graves of the mostly Black residents who were buried in one section of the cemetery without markers or any way to identify where the remains lie. As technology advances, it may be possible to determine the difference between a grave with a body in it and a grave that was dug but now has no body, without disturbing the earth.

Grave robbing was also a concern in remote family cemeteries. Velma Brinkley recalled a very wealthy man who had passed away and was buried in his best clothes with "a lot of expensive jewelry," a fact that was well-known to the small, close-knit community. "A grave robber decided to dig him up and rob the body of its valuables. Trouble was, he was ostentatious not only in his taste in jewelry but in his taste in gravestones: it was ornately carved on all sides of a square marker. The robbers didn't know which side to find the body and dug up two sides, finding nothing before abandoning the effort," laughed Brinkley.

10

A Dark and Bloody Ground

Whole Indian Nations have melted away like snowballs in the sun before the White man's advance. We had hoped that the White men would not be willing to travel beyond the mountains. Now, that hope is gone.... The same encroaching spirit will lead them upon other land of the Tsalagi [Cherokee]. *New cessions will be asked. Finally, the whole country, which the Tsalagi and their fathers have so long occupied, will be demanded, and the remnant of the Ani Yvwiya, the Real People, once so great and formidable, will be compelled to seek refuge in some distant wilderness. There, they will be permitted to stay only a short while, until they again behold the advancing banners of the same greedy host.... Should we not therefore run all risks...rather than to submit to further loss of our country? Such treaties may be alright for men who are too old to hunt or fight. As for me, I have my young warriors about me. We will hold our land.*

—Chief Draggin' Canoe, Chickamauga Tsalagi (Cherokee)

In the early 2000s, an upscale subdivision was under development in an area of Sumner County, just bordering metropolitan Nashville/Davidson County. Such a subdivision is indicative of the breakup of expansive family farms into tracts of land for single-family homes and strip shopping centers—an occurrence all over America at any given time, as large cities outgrow their boundaries and reach into the rural surrounding counties.

Families were moving into the new homes, one by one, and the process of "settling" this new subdivision was the modern equivalent of the arrival of the White man to the wilds of the new lands settled during America's westward expansion in the late 1700s. Only this time, the settlers had running water, grocery stores and schools instead of creeks and competing with Natives for food sources. They did not need to run to forts when the Natives resisted encroachment by whatever means necessary.

The young families who were settling in began experiencing strange things in their new homes—drawers opening and closing, garage doors remaining open when they were certain they had closed and locked them, odd static in appliances and, in general, things going *bump* in the night.

One young couple with a three-year-old child was having trouble getting their son to stay in his bed. He kept coming into the master bedroom in the middle of the night, complaining that someone was in his room, watching him. Certain that the boy was just adjusting to his new surroundings, the couple attempted to reassure their son by buying what was then a state-of-the-art appliance—a baby monitor that had sound and a video screen—so they could observe him in his room and soothe him back to sleep if he awoke.

The last night the couple spent in their new home, their son awoke them in the night saying there was someone in his bed. The mother looked over at the baby monitor. In her son's bed was a naked boy, about the age of her son, with long, straight hair and something that looked like beads around his neck. "An Indian boy" was the first thought that came to her mind. After waking her husband and running to her son's room, she found the bed empty.

Hollywood has found the "haunted Native burial ground" to be a convenient vehicle for horror in films—from blockbusters like *The Shining*, *Amityville Horror* and *Pet Sematary* to low-budget films, such as *Monsterwolf* and *Scalps*. Colin Dickey, in his book *Ghostland: An American History in Haunted Places*, says he believes movies like these "work" by "playing off a buried latent anxiety Americans have about the land they 'own.' If you're willing to see this conflict over land as the basis of many of our ghost stories, then it won't be surprising that so much of America is haunted."

And if bloody conflict with high casualties is a predictor of future hauntings, then Sumner County is exhibit A. Not only did the Civil War produce restless spirits there, but the fledgling United States' genocidal war against the Cherokee, who were dedicated to the defense of their land at all costs, resulted in hasty graves being dug where casualties from both sides fell throughout Middle Tennessee. Those casualties now slumber under many subdivisions, shopping centers and town squares.

Many such attacks were led by an iconic Cherokee leader who some historians have called the Red Napoleon, and he is considered the most significant American Native leader of the Southeast. Draggin' Canoe was six

Draggin' Canoe, a Cherokee warrior, was often called the Red Napoleon for his skill and bravery in fighting against the expansion of White settlers into Cherokee Territory. He fought with the British against the Continental army during the Revolutionary War and refused to surrender, even after the American victory, saying that any further conquest of Native land would result in a "dark and bloody ground." *Jim Cook, from a sculpture on display in the Elizabethton, Tennessee museum.*

feet tall and pockmarked from having contracted smallpox at a young age. Born around 1730 in Tennessee, he joined forces with the British against the Americans. And unlike some Native leaders, he refused to negotiate treaties with the victorious Americans after the Revolution, as he firmly believed that doing so would only encourage further encroachment on Native lands until there was simply nowhere else for them to go but wherever the conquerors desired them to go, thus forcing them off lands they had held for centuries.

In 1775, the largest private real estate transaction in United States history, engineered by the Transylvania Land Company, saw a whopping 20 million acres of land leave Cherokee hands for the first time in centuries. The acquisition included all of Middle Tennessee, all the lands on the Kentucky River and the entire Cumberland Watershed. Draggin' Canoe warned the purchasers that they were purchasing a "dark and bloody ground" and continued his war against the White interlopers, despite the fact that many Native leaders had ceased fighting.

In April 1788, the three sons of William Montgomery were killed near their father's house on Drake's Creek in Sumner County, three miles below Shackle Island and in the general vicinity of the subdivision that has experienced much paranormal activity. The eldest son was on crutches that day, as he had suffered a broken thigh a year before at the hands of the Natives. He was helping his brothers trim apple trees when Natives set upon the children, murdered and scalped them and then piled their bodies in a heap on a brush pile. Their graves still stand amid the modern growth and development.

At times, the Natives were not after scalps—but enslaved people. Malvina Gardner was enslaved in the early 1800s in the home of Mr. Gardner until a man named D.B. Smith saw her and, noticing the physical perfection of her, purchased her at once from her master. Malvina was aggrieved at being compelled to leave her old home and her lovely young mistress. Puss Gardner was fond of the little mulatto girl and had taught her to be a useful member of the Gardner family; however, she was sold to Mr. Smith and was compelled to accompany him to his home.

The Smith plantation was situated on the Cumberland River and commanded a beautiful view of river and valley acres, but Malvina was very unhappy and longed for her old friends back at the Gardner home. One night, the little girl gathered her few personal belongings and started back to her old home. A Native named Buck captured her, and under the laws of the tribe, Malvina became his personal property.

Malvina lived for almost a year in a teepee with Buck, and during that time, she learned much about Native habits. When Malvina was missed from her new home, Mr. Smith went to the Gardner plantation to report his loss. Not finding her there, a wide search was made for her, but the Natives kept her thoroughly concealed. Miss Puss, however, kept up the search.

The men of the Gardner plantation, White and Black, overtook the Natives and demanded the girl be given up to them. The Natives complied.

Malvina Gardner was not yet twelve years of age when she was captured by the Natives and was scarcely thirteen years of age when she became the mother of Joseph William, the son of Buck. The child was born in the Gardner home, and mother and child remained there.

Many of the atrocities committed against settler families and others like them were most likely perpetrated under the leadership or at the direction of Draggin' Canoe.

It is during this relative period, from 1788 until 1795, that Andrew Jackson was riding the circuit of county courts as both judge and counsel. Jackson made the journey of nearly two hundred miles between Nashville and Jonesboro twenty-two times; and on these occasions, there were many alarms from Indians, which sometimes grew into a forest campaign. In one of these affairs, having nearly lost his life in an adventurous feat, Jackson made the characteristic remark: "A miss is as good as a mile; you see how near I can graze danger." It was this wild experience that prepared the way for Jackson's eminence as an Indian fighter and perhaps even influenced his complicity in removing the Cherokee from the territory, as the infamous "Trail of Tears" occurred during his presidency.

In 1791, the Cherokee signed a treaty intended to end all hostilities. Draggin' Canoe, at last, agreed to participate in the treaty. The United States agreed to advance "civilization" among the Cherokee by giving them farm tools and technical support, and it promised that the land left to the Cherokee would remain theirs forever.

But in 1830:

> *Congress passed the Indian Removal Act, which required the various Indian tribes in today's southeastern United States to give up their lands in exchange for federal territory, which was located west of the Mississippi River. Most Indians fiercely resisted this policy, but as the 1830s wore on, most of the major tribes—the Choctaws, Muscogee Creeks, Seminoles, and Chickasaws—agreed to be relocated to Indian Territory* [in present-day Oklahoma]. *The Cherokee were forced to move because a small, rump faction of the tribe signed the Treaty of New Echota in late 1835, a treaty that the U.S. Senate ratified in May 1836. This action—the treaty signing and its subsequent Senate approval—tore the Cherokee into two implacable factions: a minority of those who were allied with the "treaty party," and the vast majority that bitterly opposed the treaty signing.*

In May 1838, the Cherokee removal process began. U.S. Army troops, along with various state militia, moved into the tribe's homelands and forcibly evicted more than sixteen thousand Cherokee people from their homelands in Tennessee, Alabama, North Carolina and Georgia. They were first sent to so-called round-up camps and, soon afterward, to one of three emigration camps.

Once there, the U.S. Army gave orders to move the Cherokee west. In June 1838, three detachments left southeastern Tennessee and were sent to Indian Territory by water. Difficulties with those moves, however, led to negotiations between Principal Chief John Ross and U.S. Army general Winfield Scott, and later that summer, Scott issued an order stating that Ross would oversee all future detachment movements. Ross, honoring that pledge, orchestrated the migration of fourteen detachments, most of which traveled over existing roads, between August and December 1838.

The effect of the resulting "Trail of Tears" fulfilled Draggin' Canoe's bleak prophecy. More than one thousand Cherokee—particularly the old, young and infirm—died during their trip west. Hundreds more deserted from the detachments, and an unknown number—perhaps several thousand—perished from the consequences of the forced migration. The tragic relocation was completed by the end of March 1839, and the resettlement of tribal members in Oklahoma began soon afterward.

This "dark and bloody ground" and the forced removal from sacred lands may contribute to the spirits from long ago being restless, but violence is not confined to conflict between settlers and Natives. At the site of Fort Bledsoe, not far from Cragfont, is the Cavern of the Skulls. A few hundred feet east of the old fort site is the entrance to the cavern, a mere five by ten feet. Nineteenth-century cave explorers found human skulls in the cave, which suggested inhabitants of the Cheskiki Mound Village may have used the cave to store "trophy" skulls, as a ritual scene depicted on an artifact found at the mound site shows a triumphant warrior proudly holding aloft the skull of a conquered tribesman.

The Mississippian (so named because they were located within the Mississippi River Valley) culture was the largest and most complex society living in and around the state from around 1,000 CE to 1500 CE, and they are most frequently referred to as the mound builders. They are traditionally not referred to as American Natives but are believed to have been their ancestors.

The Mississippi culture was highly structured, with two distinct classes: commoners and elites. And the burial customs reflected the status of each class.

The elites were buried in mounds, often in stone-lined tombs known as box graves. Archeologists have excavated approximately twenty-five thousand stone box graves in Middle Tennessee. The durability of the graves has facilitated the preservation of a wealth of artifacts, including fine pottery, engraved copper plates, symbolic weapons and, somewhat grimly, the remains of commoner servants who appear to have been sacrificed in order to be buried with their ruler.

Sumner County has several mounds of archeological importance located in the Castalian Springs area, where Fort Bledsoe and Cragfont are located. Some believe the presence of these mounds causes the abundance of paranormal encounters in the area and even at Cragfont itself, but the question is posited: did the ancient ones choose a site for a mound because it already had spiritual significance to them, or was the site merely convenient? Does the presence of these mounds, with their many interred bodies—some sacrificial offerings—create supernatural happenings?

"Sumner County, by the time of the westward expansion, was not home to Native American settlements; it was their hunting ground only, and tribes warred amongst themselves for the rights to that ground," said historian and artist Bill Puryear. Things were complicated when the White man became yet another contestant for these lands. Prior to approximately the year 1450, indigenous people resided in the area and had permanent settlements. But "'something' happened to warn the Natives away from permanent settlements after 1450, according to Puryear. "We can speculate that some supernatural occurrence or, to them, unexplainable and otherworldly event, such as a meteor or earthquake warned them off."

When Natives were asked by early settlers about the mounds in the area, they said they knew nothing about them that they could share, only that the "very ancient ones" constructed them—so long ago that even the oral history had been lost.

During their time in Middle Tennessee, the mound builders would have utilized the mineral waters around Castalian Springs, especially in the production of salt for ritual and culinary uses, although there is not as much evidence of the large-scale production of salt for sale and trade, as is found in other prehistoric mound builder sites in the Southeast. The Natives of eastern North America apparently used salt as a condiment. There is no evidence that salt was ever historically used for preserving meat or fish, as drying game over a low fire was the standard southeastern method of preservation. Ironically, blessed salt is often used in modern times in "cleansing" haunted homes and properties, both in Native and Catholic rituals.

Following the mound builders were the Shawnee, who were the first tribe of Natives to settle in Middle Tennessee. Other tribes formed and followed.

Whether the conflicts and killings that contribute to ghosts and spirits are the result of the ancient ones' intertribal warfare, settler-Native struggles or Civil War casualties, both troop and civilian, Sumner County has been at the historical forefront of the inevitable death and destruction that accompanies conquest, settlement and population of a new world.

As Collin Dickey wrote, "There's precious little land in the United States that hasn't been contested, one way or another through the years.... Americans live on haunted land because we have no other choice."

The ghosts, spirits and paranormal activity in Sumner County are as colorful and diverse as the people who have occupied its land for centuries and even millenia.

The origins of some of the hauntings may never be known. Others are quite obvious. There are phenomena yet to be experienced and explored, as new stories appear just when one thinks they have "heard it all."

From Cragfont's terrifying and complex paranormal activity to the sad residual spirits of a tragic American conflict and the mysterious ghost children on the public square, much is left to discover in haunted Sumner County.

BIBLIOGRAPHY

Books, Newspapers and Periodicals

Albright, Edward. *Early History of Middle Tennessee.* Nashville, TN: Brandon Printing Company, 1909.

Anderson, James Douglas. *Making the American Thoroughbred, Especially in Tennessee, 1800–1845.* Boston, MA: Plimpton Press, 1916.

Austin American-Statesman (Austin, TX). "Disastrous Fire." July 17, 1899.

Blai, Adam C. *Hauntings, Possessions, and Exorcisms.* Steubenville, OH: Emmaus Road Publishing, 2017.

Brinkley, Velma Howell. *Up From a Log Cabin, A History of First Baptist Church 1865–2003.* Clarksville, TN: Jostens Printing and Publishing, 2005.

Brown, Janet M. *Herbal Use in the American Civil War.* N.p.: Create Space Independent Publishing Platform, 2016.

Cincinnati Daily Star (Cincinnati, OH). "Disastrous Fire at Gallatin." April 20, 1880.

Cisco, Jay Guy. "Historic Sumner County." *Nashville American*, 1907.

———. *Historic Sumner County, Tennessee: Genealogies of Bledsoe, Cage and Douglas Families.* Nashville, TN: Folk-Keelin Printing Company, 1909.

Clarksville Weekly Chronicle (Clarksville, TN). "Later and Startling Discoveries in the Gallatin Cave; Another Large Quantity of Specie and Jewelry Found." June 3, 1882.

Colyar, Arthur St. Clair. *The Life and Times of Andrew Jackson.* Nashville, TN: Marshall and Bruce Company, 1904.

Cranmer, Bob, and Erica Manfred. *The Demon of Brownsville Road.* New York: Penguin Publishing Group, 2014.

Deshea, Robert. *New York Spirit of the Times*. New York: February 8, 1839.

Dickey, Collin. *Ghostland: An American History in Haunted Places.* New York: Viking Press, 2016.

Duke, Basil. *History of Morgan's Cavalry*. Cincinnati, OH: Miami Printing and Publishing Company, 1867.

Durham, Walter T. *Josephus Conn Guild and Rosemont, Politics and Plantation in Nineteenth Century Tennessee.* Nashville, TN: Hillsboro Press, 2002.

———. *Rebellion Revisited: A History of Sumner County, Tennessee from 1861 to 1870*. Nashville, Tennessee: Hillsboro Press, 1982.

Federal Writers' Project. "Ex-Slave Stories." Compiled 1936–1940.

Hallum, John. *Diary of An Old Lawyer*. Nashville, TN: Southwestern Publishing House, 1895.

Lawler, Andrew. *The Secret Token Myth, Obsession, and the Search for the Lost Colony of Roanoke.* New York: Doubleday, 2018.

Masters, Jack, William Puryear and Doug Drake. *Founding of the Cumberland Settlements*. Gallatin, TN: Warioto Press, 2009.

Mitchell, Dawn. "The Business of Body Snatching in Indianapolis." *Indianapolis Star*, May 1, 2016.

Nashville Tennessean. "Engines Sent to Gallatin." July 13, 1899.

———. "The Ghost Kept Dancing Until It Broke Its Leg." March 12, 1970.

New York Times. "Department of the Cumberland; Advance of Gen. Rosecran's Army at Gallatins, Tenn. the Place Intensely Bocesh—a Beautiful Country—Expected Advance to Murfreesboro." November 24, 1862.

Oneida, Tennessee Independent-Herald. "John Muir Walked Across the Cumberland." July 23, 2019.

Owensburg Messenger-Inquirer. "Cave of Horrors." April 23, 1907.

Schaller, Mary. *Papa Was a Boy in Gray Memories of Confederate Veterans Related by Their Living Daughters*. New York: Thomas Publishers, 2001.

Schell, Mary Robertson. *Town in Turmoil Gallatin, 1862.* Transcribed and narrated by Judith A. Morgan. Gallatin, TN: Sumner County Historical Society, 2017.

Smith, J. Frazer. *White Pillars, A Survey of Southern Dwellings of the First Half of the 1800s.* New York: Bramhall House, 1941.

Williamson, Alice (diary). Flowers Collection, William R. Perkins Library, Duke University, Durham, North Carolina.

Wills, Ridley. "The Eclipse of the Thoroughbred Horse Industry in Tennessee." *Tennessee Historical Quarterly* 46, no. 3 (1987): 157–71. www.jstor.org.

Winchester, Susan Black. *Long, Long Ago Reminiscences of Cragfont.* Gallatin, TN: Cragfont Historic Site, n.p.

Internet sources

AHGP Tennessee. "The Mound Builders, First Indian Settlers." www.tnahgp.genealogyvillage.com.

Bledsoe's Lick Historical Association. www.bledsoeslick.com.

Browsky, Richard. "Cavefishes." *Current Biology* 28, no. 2 (January 2018): R60–R64. www.sciencedirect.com.

Peach State Archaeological Society. www.peachstatearcheologicalsociety.org.

Taylor, Stephen J. "Ghoul Busters: Indianapolis Guards Its Dead (Or Does It?)" *Hoosier State Chronicles*, January 24, 2015. www.blog.newspapers.library.in.gov.

Tennessee State Library and Archive. "Tennessee Myths and Legends—Native Americans." www.sharetngov.tnsosfiles.com.

Wikisource. "The Presidents of the United States, 1789–1914/AndrewJackson." en.wikisource.org.

About the Author

Donna Lyn Hartley is a fifth-generation Texan, transplanted to Tennessee in the early 1990s.

She holds a Bachelor of Science degree in Advertising from the University of Texas at Austin and a JD from the Nashville School of Law.

Donna spent ten years as a newspaper reporter and editor in Texas; she also worked as an aide to a Texas state representative and held media-related jobs in public service and nonprofit organizations.

A lover of all things history-related, she has appeared in cemetery tours in Nashville and Gallatin and is the creator/presenter of the Gallatin Ghost Walk History and Mystery Tour.

Donna is married to attorney Randy P. Lucas and has a daughter, Rebecca, and two granddaughters, Katie and Sophie.

She is a fourth-generation member of the United Daughters of the Confederacy, Albert Sidney Johnston Chapter, in Austin, Texas.